AVIATION AND SPACE MUSEUMS OF AMERICA

AVIATION AND SPACE MUSEUMS OF AMERICA

JON L. ALLEN

TL
506
U5
A38

ARCO PUBLISHING COMPANY, INC.
219 Park Avenue South, New York, N.Y. 10003

Published by Arco Publishing Company, Inc.
219 Park Avenue South, New York, N.Y. 10003

Library of Congress Catalog Card Number 73-91258
ISBN 0-668-03426-2 (Library Edition)
ISBN 0-668-03631-1 (Paper Edition)

Printed in the United States of America

Contents

SOUTHEAST

Foreword

It would seem that there is no "right" time to publish a practical guide to aviation and space museums in North America. The only constant characteristic of the museum scene appears to be change, with the result that even the most thorough research can become outdated in less than a year.

What I have undertaken in *Aviation and Space Museums of America* is to focus on stability: to list permanent facilities now in operation which are open to the general public. Within the last several years, however, some long-established aviation museums have closed their doors for various reasons. Their directors are naturally reluctant to discuss in any detail future plans to relocate or to merge with other museums, since invariably, negotiations cannot be completed quickly and there are, undoubtedly, various alternatives to be considered.

On the other hand, the list of organizations being formed to plan and build new museums grows longer all the time. Many have made considerable progress and expect to be open to the public in another year or two. Others must make longer-range plans because formidable financial hurdles have yet to be overcome.

I am hopeful that as new museums open, I will be able to include them in later editions of this book. For the present, however, I hold the view that this guide is not so much a status report on the aviation museum scene as it is a *practical* guide. It has not been undertaken as a reference source for the enthusiast or historian, but as a general guidebook which will be of interest to anyone. Certainly, enthusiasts should also find it useful in the same sense that guidebooks to automobile, railroad, and maritime museums may be useful, though they are by no means intended to be the sole sources of information on their subjects.

It is worth mentioning several criteria which were established for this volume. As previously stated, listings are limited to facilities which are open to the general public. Private collections of aircraft or businesses engaged in the restoration and sale of vintage aircraft are purposely excluded. Nor have I attempted to include the many regional and local museums throughout the country which contain perhaps one or two aircraft or replicas even though their primary interests are not in the field of aviation.

Lists have already been compiled which locate many single aircraft, whether they are in museums or displayed in front of public buildings, in playgrounds, or at the entrance to military installations. I have chosen not to consider such displays as constituting a "collection" or a "museum."

I have been guided by my agreement with the statement made by F.C. Durant III in July, 1972, in connection with the transmittal of a report on the feasability of the Smithsonian Institution establishing an aerospace museum in the Western United States. He stated:

"The term museum was interpreted broadly to include all *permanent* institutions concerned with communicating a perception of aerospace history, science, and technology to the public visitor–user. It was found that such organizations range from classic museums with unique collections of aerospace artifacts, staffed with curator and research personnel, to public attractions which are primarily collections of antique airplanes or 'flying circus' demonstrations."

Possibly one of the most difficult tasks which I faced was that of limiting the contents of this book to existing museums and collections. There are a number of excellent collections still being formed or in storage awaiting a permanent facility in which they may be displayed. There are organizations which have accomplished much towards realizing the establishment of new museums. Yet, restraint has been the overriding consideration in providing the reader with useful, rather than speculative, guidance on the aviation and space museum scene as it exists at the present time.

Jon Allen
New York, New York

Acknowledgments

One of the real pleasures of undertaking a project such as *Aviation and Space Museums of America* is derived from the many warm relationships which develop with so many people with similar interests.

Without exception, those who have assisted during the research for this volume, provided photographs, or made suggestions have done so with unfailing goodwill and generosity.

I am deeply indebted to many longstanding friends and colleagues for their encouragement and counsel, as well as to the many individuals who provided information about the museums listed, museums no longer open to the public, and museums which have yet to open.

My particular thanks go to Colonel John W. Walton, Miss Karen A. Conley, Frank Gudaitis, Alvin E. Sherman, Colonel John W. Hinds, Albert Zuckerman, Frank Strnad, Peter Miller, and Irving H. Breslauer.

Also, thanks to Jay Miller, Ted Tate, Miss Page Shamberger, David R. Winans, Chapin R. Leinbach, Miss Peggy Welch, Harvey Katz, Miss Althea Lister, Frank Doherty, and Major Shirley Bach.

My appreciation is also due to each and every museum director, public affairs officer, aviation historian, and curator who provided information and illustrations. My thanks to:

Harvey H. Lippincott, Bill McLaughlin, Miss Claudia M. Oakes, John Whitelaw, Daniel E. O'Brien, John H. Talmage, Cole Palen, Merrill Stickler, William D. English, Jr., Albert D. Hollingsworth, Lieutenant Commander L.J. Sheya, James G. Craig, William A. Howell, Miss Doris R. Hunter, Edward O. Buckbee, Arthur B. Hicks, Dale D. Reed, Norman G. Messinger, Thomas C. Griffin, M.A. Richardson, Franklin R. Roach, Major C.A. Fleming, Miss Emma-Jo L. Davis, Dr. Robert D. Helton, John U. Wyer, Warren M. Bolon, and Earl Reinert.

Also, John C. Lord, Stephen F. Stein, Robert L. Taylor, J. Robert Dawson, Harold Warp, Carol A. Janssen, A. Joseph Zawatski, Mrs. Philip L. Sommerlad, Mrs. Hubert A. Miller, Colonel John E. Condron, R.E. Baughman, Walter A. Soplata, Miss Kathy Minkin, Rhodes Arnold, Sergeant Robert M. Meraim, Gabriel J. Brillante, Carroll V. Canfield, Mrs. Kathryn E. McCray, Mrs. Gloria M. Livingston, Colonel Glenn Bercot, Jim Peel, Paul M. Sturtevant, Commander W.R. Tully, Lieutenant Commander R.D. McEwen, Colonel Owen F. Clarke, Jack Goins, David P. Johnson, Clay Henley, Mark Curtis, Tad Dunbar, J.D. Forney, Miss Katita Stark, and Stanley G. Reynolds.

And, Lee R. Embree, Colonel E.F. Carey, Jr., Bill Hodges, Paul H. Poberezny, Captain Grover Walker, Lieutenant Commander Paul N. Mullane, Greg Killingsworth, Rick Kiefer, David R. Huffman, Shelby B. Hagberg, Miss Dianne Rose, Robert Dodsley, Bob Gardner, John A. Puravs, J. Roger Bentley, W.G. Hamner, Bernie Nellis, Dr. John P. Roberts, Adrian Delfino, Marvin K. Hand, Mrs. Dody Engel, Robert Stapp, William D. Ross, Bill Robinson, Ken Turpin, Miss Linda G. Cole, Don Sarno, William J. Wheeler, Kenneth M. Molson, Art Romeo, James Brucker, Ed Maloney, William R. Davenport, John L. Sherwin, Delbert W. Kindschi, Major William F. Frensley, and Lieutenant Thomas M. Weaver, Lou Davis, Rev. John Frizzell, Ira Menefee, Stephen Hoffman, John M. Goodwin, Lieutenant Joseph H. Mills, and Robert C. Reiley.

NORTHEAST

Transport planes which are open to visitors at the Bradley Air
Museum include a Lockheed 749A Constellation and, behind it, a
Douglas C–124 Globemaster. (Photo by Lewis R. Berlepsch.)

Bradley Air Museum
Windsor Locks, Connecticut

Unique in the New England states, the Bradley Air Museum is situated in an area with a long aviation heritage. It is the home of several leading aerospace firms which have produced many "firsts" in the industry.

The beginnings of the museum can be traced to 1959 and the formation of the Connecticut Aeronautical Historical Association. Within two years, the group (which today numbers over 400 members) had decided that formation of a museum would be the best way to preserve the area's aviation heritage. The museum, which is operated entirely by the Association, opened its doors to the public in May, 1968, on a 3.93-acre site at Bradley International Airport.

The aircraft collection includes a total of 39 airplanes, three balloons, 10 helicopters, five unmanned aircraft, and one rocket—for a total of 58. They are divided into four groups for fighters, bombers, transports, and vertical lift.

The museum also has an aircraft engine collection, and its total of 73 engines is the third largest in the United States. An important group of Pratt & Whitney engines is included, along with piston, turbine, and rocket engines of different periods, as well as Connecticut's oldest aircraft engine, a 1909 Smith engine built in Hartford, Conn.

The Connecticut Aeronautical Historical Association also maintains a collection of memorabilia about New England aviation pioneers and events, as well as archives containing some 2000 books and an additional 4000 documents, brochures, and texts.

Although the entire museum is outdoors, visitors may enter a number of the larger aircraft in which the organization has erected "mini-museums" about particular aspects of aviation and flight. Future plans do call for the construction of permanent buildings, though in the interim a small metal hangar serves to house material on the history of aeronautics. One additional building houses the ticket counter and a small souvenir shop, built to serve the more than 26,000 visitors who come to the museum each year.

Among the principal aircraft on display are well-preserved commercial and military transport planes which may be viewed inside as well. These include the Lockheed 14 Super Electra; the Lockheed Constellation; the Douglas C–54D Skymaster, military version of the DC–4 and backbone of the Berlin Airlift; the Fairchild C–119 Packet, which was used for paratroop drops; a Douglas C–124 Globemaster; and a giant Douglas C–133 Cargomaster.

Aircraft in the fighter group include the Chance Vought F4U Corsair, Convair F–102 Delta Dagger, and Grumman F9F–2 Panther, as well as a North American FJ–1 Fury, North American F–86 Sabre, North American F–100 Super Sabre, Northrop F–89 Scorpion, and Republic RF–84F Thunderflash. A Lockheed T–33A trainer is also in this section. Bombers in the inventory include the Boeing B–17G and Boeing B–47E, along with a Lockheed SP–2E Neptune. The helicopters on display are the Sikorsky UH–19D Chickasaw and the Sikorsky CH–37B Mojave. A specimen of the standard air-sea rescue amphibian used for a number of years by the Air Force and Coast Guard, the Grumman HU–16B Albatross, is also on exhibit.

All of the outdoor displays are of relatively modern aircraft, since some of the museum's earlier and most interesting items are in storage until permanent quarters can be constructed in which to house them. In this category is the collection's balloon *Jupiter,* built by Silas Brooks in 1886, and the oldest surviving aircraft in the United States. Other items are a Bunce–Curtiss Pusher of 1912, a Fokker Universal Transport of 1928, the Gee Bee sports plane of 1930, a Laird Solution

Some 30 different transports, fighters, bombers, and special-purpose aircraft are displayed at the Bradley Air Museum. (Photo by Lewis R. Berlepsch.

racer of 1930, and an early amphibian, the Sikorsky S–39 of 1930.

Membership in the Connecticut Aeronautical Historical Association is open to anyone interested in aviation history and details can be obtained from Harvey H. Lippincott, director of the museum, at P.O. Box 44, Hebron, Connecticut 06248. The Association publishes a quarterly newsletter and annual membership dues start at $7.00.

Location: The Bradley Air Museum is on the east side of Bradley International Airport at Windsor Locks, Connecticut, about midway between Hartford, Connecticut and Springfield, Massachusetts. From Interstate 91, motorists should exit on Route 20, then turn north on Route 75 as far as the third traffic light. After a left turn, signs indicate the way to the museum. Ample free parking is available.

Schedule: Open Saturdays, Sundays, and holidays, except on Christmas Day, weather permitting, from 10 a.m. to 6 p.m. Also open weekdays from June through September from 10 a.m. to 6 p.m.

Admission: $1.00 for adults, 50 cents for children. Free for preschool children and members of the Connecticut Aeronautical Historical Association. Special rate for youth groups of 25 cents each.

Gemini capsule in which Astronaut Edward H. White II became the first man to "walk" in space. Also exhibited at the Smithsonian is Astronaut John Glenn's "Friendship VII" in which he became the first American to circle the earth. (Courtesy of the Smithsonian Institution.)

National Air and Space Museum
Smithsonian Institution
Washington, D.C.

Already outstanding and scheduled to become bigger and better during the nation's bicentennial year, the National Air and Space Museum of the Smithsonian Institution ranks among the best aviation museums in the world.

The display techniques and resources available to the museum staff enable them to mount some of the best-conceived and most fascinating aviation and space exhibits to be seen in the country. Visitors never need to worry about repeating at the Smithsonian as there is always something new, with exhibits rotated on a regular basis. Many of the National Aviation and Space Museum's specimens are unique and, as an official repository, the Smithsonian has long received original items which must be reproduced to be displayed elsewhere.

Despite the modern aspect of some of the more popular space age exhibits, it should be remembered that the Smithsonian's involvement with aviation goes back as early as 1861, when Joseph Henry, the Institution's first secretary, recommended to President Lincoln that balloons be used for aerial reconnaissance during the Civil War.

The Smithsonian started to accumulate its aeronautical collection at the time of the 1876 Philadelphia Centennial Exposition when a group of kites was acquired from the Chinese Imperial Commission. Samuel P. Langley, the

Institution's third secretary, conducted aerodynamic experiments from 1887 to 1903 that resulted in the successful flights of a number of unmanned "aerodromes."

In 1915, the Smithsonian established a National Advisory Committee for Aeronautics, and two years later, Dr. Robert H. Goddard was granted research funds for his experiments in rocket propulsion.

To display the specimens in its growing aeronautical collection, the Smithsonian acquired a temporary World War I building in 1920 which provided more space than was available in the Arts and Industries Building. The Smithsonian had acquired its first Wright Brothers airplane in 1911, the Wright Flyer A, first military aircraft in the world.

In 1948, the original 1903 Wright Brothers aircraft was presented to the Smithsonian by the executors of Orville Wright's estate at his specific request.

Congress officially established the National Air Museum as a bureau of the Smithsonian Institution in 1946. Twenty years later that act was amended to include space flight, and the museum was charged with the responsibility of preserving the heritage of aviation and space flight.

In 1976, the National Air and Space Museum is scheduled to move to new quarters in a spacious building on the Mall in Washington, between 4th and 7th Streets. With 633,000 square feet of exhibit space, it will contain 20 halls on four levels. The $42 million structure will be unquestionably the finest facility of its type anywhere in the world, with more than adequate space to display the National Aeronautical Collections.

In addition to the quarters currently in use in Washington, the National Air and Space Museum has workshops and storage space at Silver Hill, Maryland, where restoration work is conducted and rotating exhibits are stored.

At present, the museum's collection is divided between the old Arts and Industries Building, constructed in 1879, and the temporary building behind the Smithsonian's offices. In the main building, one may see the original Wright Brothers 1903 Flyer, Charles A. Lindbergh's *Spirit of St. Louis,* the Apollo XI command module, the Mercury VII spacecraft, and a sample of lunar rock collected by Astronaut Neil Armstrong, the first man to walk on the moon.

A World War I airdrome in the Smithsonian has a Spad VII
suspended in the foreground, General Billy Mitchell's Spad XVI
behind it, and a Fokker D–VII below. Sound effects help recreate
the atmosphere of the Western front. (Courtesy of the Smithsonian
Institution.)

It's also in this building that special exhibits are mounted periodically. Among these have been a World War I airdrome, complete with tape recorded conversations coming from inside temporary buildings, uniforms, decorations, and memorabilia. A Fokker D–VII stands near a sandbagged gun emplacement and a Spad VII and the original Spad XVI flown by General Billy Mitchell are suspended from the ceiling.

Other special exhibits have included one on ballooning, and others on aerobatic flying, air traffic control, and aircraft engines. A selection of paintings from the U.S. Air Force art collection is exhibited on the balcony, and a case near the *Spirit of St. Louis* contains Charles A. Lindbergh's personal flying suit, navigation equipment, logbooks, and other items carried on his solo transatlantic flight.

Also in the Arts and Industries Building is a most comprehensive bookshop, containing titles on every branch of aeronautics, astronautics, aerial warfare, and space flight. An aviation enthusiast could start a respectable library during a single visit, and there are posters, models, and dozens of souvenirs for sale.

Between the Arts and Industries Building and the Air and Space Building stand a row of missiles which easily catch the eyes of the more than two million people who visit the Smithsonian every year. They include a Jupiter C, the Vanguard, a Polaris, and the Atlas.

A walk through the Air and Space Building enables visitors to see many aspects of aviation and space flight, with strong emphasis on historic achievements. There are wall panels and display cases on aviation pioneers, early first flights over the poles and oceans, and on goodwill flights. Similar exhibits cover the role of women in aviation, the development of parachutes, airmail pioneers, dirigibles, and ballooning.

Notable aircraft on display are Wiley Post's *Winnie Mae,* the Lockheed Vega 5–C in which he circumnavigated the world twice; the *Vin Fiz,* a Wright biplane in which Calbraith Perry Rodgers made the first coast-to-coast flight; and the Bell X–1, first aircraft to fly faster than sound.

In a modern vein, youngsters can try their hands at a spacecraft docking maneuver. As they move the controls, models simulate their commands while they sit in a realistic capsule.

Suspended from the roof of the Smithsonian Institution is Charles A. Lindbergh's original *Spirit of St. Louis* in which he made the first transatlantic solo crossing on May 20, 1927 in 33 hours. (Courtesy of the Smithsonian Institution.)

The National Air and Space Museum's collection far exceeds the space which has been available in which to exhibit it. Many exhibits, suspended from the ceiling or crowded beside others, have not been displayed adequately. This was recognized some years ago, with the new site for the museum designated as early as 1958 and funds appropriated for its design in 1970.

According to Astronaut Michael Collins, who serves as director of the museum, the new facility will satisfy scientists, historians, astronomers, and aviation buffs equally, as well as "helping the lay visitor evaluate the impact air and space history and technology have had on our lives."

Location: In the center of Washington, D.C. on the south side of the Mall, the Smithsonian Institution's Arts and Industries Building and an adjacent temporary building will house the National Air and Space Museum collection until dedication of the museum's new home on July 4, 1976. The Arts and Industries building is between 9th Street and 14th Street.

Schedule: Open daily 10 a.m. to 5:30 p.m. seven days a week. Closed on Christmas Day.

Admission: Free.

The National Soaring Museum is in an old manor house owned by Chemmung County, New York. The Soaring Society of America's library and film archives are associated with the museum. (Courtesy of the National Soaring Museum.)

National Soaring Museum
Elmira, New York

With the emphasis in most aviation and space museums on powered flight, a trip to Harris Hill, New York, is a refreshing change of pace. The National Soaring Museum, which opened here in July, 1969, occupies a spacious manor house loaned to the organization by Chemung County. It's a fascinating museum.

The museum occupies about 4000 square feet of space and maintains a library. Its location here (at the initiative of the Soaring Society of America) was a natural choice, for the Elmira area has been known as the "soaring capital of America" since the nation's first national contests were held here in 1930.

Soaring is generally acknowledged to have had its beginnings in 1855, when a French officer made the first glider flight. During the 1890s Otto Lilienthal made numerous flights, and soaring became important in America during the same period.

In fact, the diverse popularity of the sport may be measured by the contrast between one of the nation's first enthusiasts and one of its most recent. Octave Chanute made his first flight in 1896 at the age of 64 and subsequently made some 2000 accident-free flights. Neil A. Armstrong, first man on the moon, has also made many flights and has qualified for his Gold Badge by completing a five hour flight, attaining a climb of 9843 feet, and covering at least 187 miles in a sailplane. He's among the less than 500 sailplane pilots in the United States who have earned the Gold Badge International Soaring Award.

The museum is filled with a wealth of artifacts—models, instruments, awards, and badges—as well as posters and mementos from numerous international competitions. Of special interest to young visitors is the full-scale sailplane cockpit in which they can climb and work the controls.

The National Soaring Museum is located within a 330-acre complex, complete with woods and picnic facilities, which is maintained by Chemung County. Incorporated within the museum's facilities are the National Soaring Library, the National Soaring Archives, the Soaring Society of America film archives, and the Diamond Badge Hall.

Early gliders owned by the museum include a 1906 Arnot, a 1906 Chanute-type, a 1929 Primary, a duPont Minimoa, a 1945 1–19 Prototype, and a 1933 Bowlus duPont Albatross. Due to space limitations, most of the fully assembled sailplanes are in storage.

Plans are underway, through a fund raising program, to provide a larger, permanent building for the museum in which full-sized sailplanes, winches, and other equipment can be exhibited.

The museum derives support from the Soaring Society of America, which in turn is composed of some 235 clubs from coast to coast, with approximately 10,000 members. Two of the 60 or so commercial soaring operators in the United States are located close to the museum: the Harris Hill Soaring Corporation and the Schweizer Aircraft Corporation and Soaring School. Both have been instrumental in sponsoring numerous meets and competitions at Harris Hill and in supporting the museum.

The well-arranged displays in the National Soaring Museum are designed to show the story of powerless flight and man's use of thermal currents to travel great distances aloft. Soaring pre-dates powered flight and, even in the space age, has its devoted enthusiasts. Never adaptable to commercial or military uses, it remains a consummate sport with increasing nationwide popularity.

Location: Harris Hill is about eight miles west of Elmira,

The National Soaring Museum has 4000 feet of display space at Harris Hill. Several aircraft are stored in a nearby hanger awaiting construction of a permanent facility. (Photo by Richard R. Hosenfeld.)

New York. Motorists on Route 17 should exit at Exit 51 and follow the signs indicating the museum location.

Schedule: 11 a.m. to 5 p.m. The museum is open on Saturdays and Sundays only from May 15 to June 14, and from September 30 to November 30. From June 15 to September 30, it is open seven days a week.

Admission: 75 cents for adults and 35 cents for children ages 12 to 18.

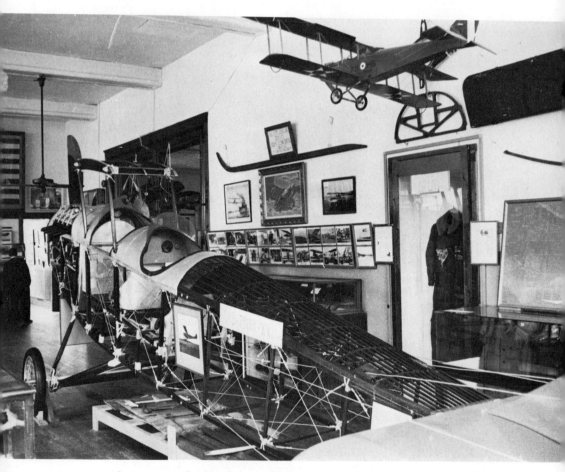

The exposed fuselage of a Curtiss JN–4 Jenny reveals its construction features to visitors to the Glenn H. Curtiss Museum at Hammondsport, N.J. The Jenny, with OX–5 engine, stands amid memorabilia of Curtiss' career. (Photo by Frank Strnad.)

Glenn H. Curtiss Museum
Hammondsport, New York

Glenn Hammond Curtiss was born in the quiet village of Hammondsport, New York, in May, 1878. It was here that he started his own bicycle shop as a teenager and, at the age of 23, became the manufacturer of some of the finest motorcycles of the day.

However, to anyone familiar with aviation, that was merely a prelude to his remarkable career designing and building aircraft and engines, many of which are preserved in his birthplace and in aviation museums throughout the world.

The Glenn H. Curtiss Museum was founded in 1960 by residents of the community who had long felt that such a facility was needed. A former school building with 12,600 square feet of display area was renovated and formation of the present collection began. By the early 1970s, an aviation library and archives were added and the museum has since become an invaluable source of research material for aviation historians.

The moving force behind the establishment and growth of the museum was the late Otto P. Kohl, who served as director and curator until 1972. Mr. Kohl came to Hammondsport in 1915 from Rochester, N.Y., where he had been a tool and die maker for the Eastman Kodak Company. He joined the Curtiss Aeroplane Motor Company in Hammondsport, worked in Buffalo during World War I, and returned to

Hammondsport in 1919. He subsequently worked for Keuka Industries, Aerial Service Corporation, Airships Incorporated, and the Meadowcroft Balloon Company. He retired from Mercury Aircraft Company in 1960 as plant supervisor, and devoted the rest of his life to the Curtiss Museum until his death in November, 1973.

To start with, the museum had one Curtiss motorcycle and one OX-5 engine. Today, there are a total of 48 engines in the collection, including almost every variation of the OX–5 Curtiss engine, as well as other engines dating from before World War I up to a modern Pratt & Whitney J–48 jet engine. The museum also houses the OX–5 Club of the Aviation Pioneer Hall of Fame. In the field of naval aviation history, the museum made a significant acquisition several years ago in the glass plate slide collection of Lieutenant Harry Benner who was responsible for much of the photographic coverage of early aviation.

A primary objective of the museum is to provide a full picture of the Hammondsport area as a center of aviation pioneering. In addition to the nine aircraft on display, much memorabilia of Curtiss' own accomplishments and those of other fliers is on exhibit, along with items depicting local history. These include special collections of early radio equipment, steamboating on Lake Keuka, and a number of items related to the local wine industry.

The aircraft in the collection include a Curtiss JN–4D of 1915, uncovered to show details of its construction; a Curtiss Model E of 1911, reconstructed from many original parts; a Curtiss Robin of 1927, also uncovered to show construction of the fuselage; and a Curtiss Oriole of 1919.

Also included are a Mercury Chick of 1929, displayed complete with the wings uncovered to illustrate its unique construction; a homebuilt racing plane of 1958; and a target drone of World War II. There are also two gliders in the collection: a Doppel Rabb glider built in Germany in the 1930s, and a Schweizer 1–19 glider of 1947.

Glenn H. Curtiss' contributions to aviation started, surprisingly, with the building of engines for pre-World War I balloons. Between 1904 and 1908, powered balloons were highly popular and, between 1901 and 1908, Curtiss' work force grew from three men to more than 100. He was a founder, along with Alexander Graham Bell, F.W. Baldwin, J.A.D. McCurdy, and Lieutenant Thomas Selfridge, of the Aerial Experiment Association, headquartered at Hammondsport. Several flights of pioneering aircraft, such as the *Red Wing, White Wing,* and *June Bug* were made in 1908, and these were followed by Curtiss' *Silver Dart, Gold Bug,* and *Golden Flyer.* In 1911, Curtiss was awarded the first pilot's license issued in America.

The Curtiss JN–4 Jenny was produced in large quantities during World War I and in the years immediately following, with some 6000 being built. A Curtiss NC–4 flying boat, commanded by Lieutenant Commander Albert C. Read, made the first transatlantic crossing by air in May, 1919. Curtiss' post-war career illustrated his varied interests. He played a part in the development of the towns of Miami Springs and Hialeah, Florida. Today, his home at the edge of Miami's International Airport is part of a hotel complex and has been used by at least one major airline for stewardess training.

It is somewhat difficult to imagine today that this quiet town in the Finger Lakes region was once a bustling center of early aviation. But, within the Glenn H. Curtiss Museum the memory of the pioneers is preserved through this tribute of the community to the man who made Hammondsport "the cradle of aviation."

Location: The Glenn H. Curtiss Museum is located at the corner of Lake and Main Streets in the town of Hammondsport. The entrance is on Lake Street and there is ample parking space available behind the building. Hammondsport is at the south end of Lake Keuka in upstate New York, about 40 miles north of Elmira on Route 15.

Schedule: 10 a.m. to 3:30 p.m. from May 1 through October 31. Open Monday through Saturday, including legal holidays, but closed Sundays. Closed in winter.

Admission: $1.00 for adults, 50 cents for children ages 7 through 12. Special rates and arrangements are available for school and other tour groups.

Antique aircraft at Old Rhinebeck range from 1908 to 1937. Out of Cole Palen's collection of 37 aircraft, 18 are in flying condition. (Photo by Jon Allen.)

Old Rhinebeck Aerodrome
Rhinebeck, New York

When Roosevelt Field in Mineola, Long Island, closed in 1948, Cole Palen acquired his first six vintage aircraft, the nucleus of a collection which today numbers almost three dozen. The most remarkable thing about the collection housed at Old Rhinebeck Aerodrome is that more than half are still flying regularly.

In 1958, Palen bought the abandoned farm on which he was to carve out a small grass airstrip, build hangars, and later add spectator seating for several thousand customers. With a judicious blend of devotion, enterprise, and "show business" sense, he has created an authentic World War I aerodrome which draws several thousand visitors every weekend from May through October. Palen and his fellow pilots, most of them teachers or engineers during the week, don German, British, French, and American uniforms of the 1914–1918 war for the occasion. Then they take off in the Sopwiths, Fokkers, Spads, and Nieuports to put on an exciting low-level aerial show, complete with running commentary on the exploits of the pernicious "Black Baron," a part Palen plays himself. Both prior to the air show and while it's going on, the vintage automobiles, trucks, and artillery pieces below are manned by costumed amateurs partaking in the scenario.

Needless to say, Old Rhinebeck Aerodrome has become a favorite location for advertising photography, television

Two hangars at the top of the hill near Old Rhinebeck Aerodrome contain non-flying aircraft, engines, paintings, and other aviation artifacts. (Photo by Jon Allen.)

Air shows on Saturday and Sunday afternoons attract thousands of spectators to Old Rhinebeck Aerodrome. Uniforms and costumes of pilots and the supporting cast on the ground are all authentic World War I era items. (Photo by Jon Allen.)

programs, and filmmakers, and the World War I aircraft and part-time actors have appeared in numerous commercials and educational programs.

Come the last weekend in October, the weekend air shows, which are held every Saturday and Sunday, finish for the season and Palen and his wife, Rita, move to Florida for the winter to rebuild more airplanes and renovate memorabilia for the museum.

While the air shows bring weekly excitement to Old Rhinebeck Aerodrome and always delight the large number of youngsters who attend, there is also much to be seen in the two museum buildings and seven hangars on the property. The aircraft which are not in flying condition are displayed here, together with engines, propellors, paintings, and other artifacts.

It's a good idea to arrive early for the Saturday and Sunday shows because of the heavy traffic. However, there are picnic tables near the airstrip, refreshment stands, and a gift shop in which to browse and pick up posters, models, books, and souvenirs.

The aircraft which fly at Old Rhinebeck are either authentic originals or accurate copies powered by original engines, and the smell of castor oil hangs heavy in the air as they roar down the runway.

Aircraft in flying condition which are owned either by Palen or by his fellow pilots include a Fokker D–VII of 1918 and a replica of a Fokker DR–1, built in 1965; a Sopwith Pup; an Aeronca C–3; a Curtiss JN–4 Jenny and Curtiss–Wright Jr. CW1; an Avro 504K; a Bleriot X1 of 1910; a Bird CK; an F.E. 8 and Fleet Finch 16B; and a Short S–29. Also included are a Thomas–Morse S4B of 1917, a Funk B; a Piper J2 Taylor Cub, Taylorcraft BC65, a Waco 9 of 1926, and a Waco 10 of 1928.

Either on static display in the museum and hangars or undergoing restoration are a 1908 Voisin; 1911 Thomas Pusher I and 1912 Thomas Pusher II; the 1918 Standard J–1; a Spad XIII; a Sopwith Snipe 7F1; a Siemens Schuckert D–III; a replica of the Santos-Dumont Demoiselle, built in 1965; a DeHavilland Puss Moth of 1930; a Breguet biplane of 1911; and a Nieuport 28 of 1917.

Also on display are a Passett Ornithopter, a Curtiss Pusher D, an Aeromarine 39B of 1918 and an Aeromarine–Klemm of

1930, an Albatross D.Va, a Monocoupe 113 of 1929, and a Raab–Katzenstein glider of 1921.

Location: Old Rhinebeck Aerodrome is at the intersection of Norton and Stone Church Roads, north of the town of Rhinebeck, close to Red Hook, New York. Stone Church Road can be reached on Route 9, north of Rhinebeck; Norton Road can be reached on Route 199 east of Red Hook. For visitors using the Taconic State Parkway, the exit to Route 199 should be used; from the New York State Thruway, Exit 19 leads across the Hudson River to Route 9. There is always ample free parking available at Old Rhinebeck Aerodrome.

Schedule: The aerodrome is open to visitors daily from 10 a.m. to 5 p.m., from May 15 through October. Aerial shows are given every Sunday throughout the season at 2:30 p.m., and every Saturday from July through October at 2:30 p.m.

Admission: $1.00 for adults and 50 cents for children, Monday through Friday. For the Saturday air shows admission is $2.00 for adults and 50 cents for children. For the Sunday air shows admission is $3.00 for adults and $1.00 for children. Pre-show activity starts at 2 p.m.

Warm weekends bring classic aircraft enthusiasts to Riverhead, N.Y. at the end of Long Island, where John H. Talmage's private airstrip and 4320-square-foot hangar are "home" to a growing vintage aircraft collection. (Photo by Frank Gudaitis.)

Talmage Field Aircraft Collection
Riverhead, New York

John H. Talmage is one of those singular men whose love of aviation has led him to form a growing collection of vintage aircraft which he is happy to share with any and all "aviation enthusiasts, historians, and young people with a keen interest in pre-jet-age aviation."

Aviation occupies a significant place in his earliest recollections. As a child, he read everything he could get his hands on about flying, built scale models and, in 1946, at the age of 16, soloed in a Piper J–3.

Graduation from college and service in the U.S. Army as a field artillery officer deferred his pursuit of fine aircraft until his return to his family farm on Long Island, of which he is now manager.

The Talmage Aircraft Collection started seriously in 1967 with the acquisition of a 1929 Arrow Sport A–2 biplane and, since then, half a dozen additional aircraft have been added, as well as various engines, propellors, wheels, instruments, and other "odds and ends."

During good weather, Mr. Talmage's flyable aircraft are joined on weekends by the craft of fellow enthusiasts who arrive at his private airport, known as *Talmage Field,* for which a portion of the farm has been set aside.

In mid-1973, a 4320-square-foot metal hangar was erected to house Mr. Talmage's aircraft. The 1929 Arrow Sport A–2 and his 1929 Travel Air 4000 are both in flyable condition. A 1940 Rearwin Cloudster and 1929 Travel Air 2000 are being rebuilt, as is a 1931 Brunner Wunkle CK Bird. Mr. Talmage designed and built his own hovercraft in 1966 and 1967. With two seats, it is powered by a McCulloch 72-horsepower engine.

In addition to the aircraft which Mr. Talmage has brought together for the first time in his new hangar, engines which may be seen include: a 1918 Curtiss OX–5, 90 horsepower; a 1918 Hispano-Suiza, 180 horsepower; a 1918 Curtiss OXX–6, 100 horsepower; a 1930 LeBlond, 60 horsepower; a 1941 Curtiss–Wright J 6–7 Whirlwind R–760–8; a 1941 Continental R–670, 220 horsepower; and a 1941 Kinner B–54, 125 horsepower.

Like many aviation enthusiasts, Mr. Talmage does not consider his Riverhead, New York, facility to be a formal "museum" although he is personally available, with advance notice, to meet with individuals or groups interested in viewing the collection. His modest library of aviation books, manuals, illustrations, and magazines is available to researchers and historians.

Location: The Talmage Field Aircraft Collection is located at Friar's Head Farm on the south side of Sound Avenue, five miles north of Riverhead, Long Island. From Exit 73 on the Long Island Expressway, motorists should take Route 58 about one mile to Mill Road, which joins Osborne Avenue, then turn right on to Sound Avenue for about one-third of a mile.

Schedule: No specific hours. On weekends a number of visiting antique aircraft are generally on hand during warm weather. Anyone interested in viewing the aircraft collection may arrange to do so by making prior arrangements. Telephone: (516) 727-0124.

Admission: Free. Donations towards maintenance of the collection are appreciated, including pre-jet books, magazines, photographs, and memorabilia.

The Franklin Institute
Philadelphia, Pennsylvania

The Franklin Institute is one of the nation's oldest museums, closely associated with scientific achievements and technical research, the latter through its affiliated Franklin Institute Research Laboratories.

Founded in 1824, it long occupied a building constructed in 1825 on Seventh Street which today houses the Atwater Kent Museum. The Franklin Institute has been located in its present 215,000 square foot building since 1959. It contains over 500 different exhibits.

The Institute's association with aviation dates from the early days of flight and its rare book room contains the complete engineering notebooks, sketches, and plans of the Wright Brothers' first airplane, given to the museum by Orville Wright, long a member of the Franklin Institute.

However, the museum's 5600-square-foot Hall of Aviation is filled with numerous exhibits which, rather than reflecting the museum's age, are designed to appeal to the numerous youngsters who visit it each year. There are exhibits in which they can sit, operate controls, and test their skills; instruments actually work, lights flash, and moving parts instruct visitors about the principles of flight. The artifacts and displays appeal equally to aviation historians and to pupils and there is indeed something in the Hall of Aviation for every member of the family.

An Air Force T–33 in which they can sit is popular with young visitors to the Hall of Aviation at the Franklin Institute. (Courtesy of the Franklin Institute.)

In addition to the Wright Brothers material housed in the rare book room, there are also several display cases of memorabilia which are available to the public. There are a total of five wind tunnels, one an operable Collins wind tunnel which is used for demonstrations, another a replica of the original Wright Brothers' wind tunnel with the original balances in place. The other three wind tunnels may be operated by visitors and they are equipped with instructions on how to determine lift, drag, and the advantages of streamlined design.

The Wright Brothers' thirteenth aircraft, a Model B biplane of 1911, is suspended from the ceiling. Completely restored, it made its last flight in 1934 on the thirty-first anniversary of the Wright Brothers' first flight.

In the center of the Hall of Aviation is an Air Force T–33 jet trainer in which visitors may sit and operate the controls. Nearby are two Link trainers which visitors may actually "fly." The museum has a monthly contest, which has been held since 1946, in which persons under 21 years of age can test their skills. Winners are awarded a pair of golden wings and an hour of free flight instruction at a nearby airport, sponsored by Exxon.

One other aircraft, a Boeing–Boelkow B–105, is on exhibit, as are a number of aircraft engines ranging from an early Anzani to jet engines used to power the modern Phantom. The Boeing–Boelkow twin jet helicopter was donated to the museum, and the parts and interiors were installed by Boeing Vertol employees on their own time during evenings and on weekends. It was presented to the museum at a dinner meeting of the local chapter of the American Helicopter Society. It features controls that operate, rotors that turn, and lights that flash as youngsters sit in the cockpit.

As one enters the Hall of Aviation, 60 feet of display cases trace the evolution of flight by lighter-than-air and heavier-than-air craft from boomerang to space shuttle. A total of more than 200 scale models are displayed, backed by panels which highlight the story of aviation and space flight. The space age is represented in the main hall by a mockup of a Mercury space capsule.

The Franklin Institute occupies almost a full city block and has a science museum and planetarium, a lecture hall, and a

The corridor leading to the Hall of Aviation traces the history of flight with illustrations and models. There are about 200 models in the collection. (Courtesy of the Franklin Institute.)

lunchroom and restaurant. It also houses the Benjamin Franklin National Memorial, which was formally dedicated in 1974.

Other sections of the Institute contain exhibits on communications, meteorology, atomic energy, optics, printing, maritime history, and other subjects.

The Franklin Institute Research Laboratories conduct contract research in various fields, including the physical sciences, mechanical and nuclear engineering, transportation, communications, environmental resources, and pollution control.

Location: The Franklin Institute is located in the center of Philadelphia at 20th Street and the Benjamin Franklin Parkway. No public parking is available, except on Saturdays and Sundays.

Schedule: Open daily from 10 a.m. to 5 p.m. Open Sundays from noon to 5 p.m. Closed on Christmas Eve, Christmas Day, New Year's Day, and Thanksgiving Day.

Admission: $1.50 for adults, $1.00 for children under 12. An additional 25 cents is charged for admission to the planetarium. Group rates are available upon request. Telephone: (215) 448-1201.

Aircraft on display at Willow Grove Naval Air Station include a
Messerschmitt ME-262, a Jill 12 torpedo bomber, and U.S. Navy
YF2Y-1 Sea Dart. (Photo by Jon Allen.)

Willow Grove Naval Air Station
Willow Grove, Pennsylvania

Although it is not officially listed as a museum facility, the small collection of aircraft displayed at the U.S. Naval Air Station at Willow Grove, Pennsylvania, is maintained in excellent condition. Since they are exhibited out of doors in an enclosed area near the edge of the base, they are constantly available for public viewing.

Willow Grove NAS serves primarily as a Naval and Marine reserve base, with U.S. Air Force and Air National Guard units also conducting flying operations there. The base was acquired in 1941 when the Navy purchased Pitcairn Airfield from Harold Pitcairn, creator of the autogiro. Additional acreage was purchased in 1957, bringing the total to about 1000 acres. Some 6000 reservists use the base every month.

The nine aircraft displayed are particularly interesting, especially those of German and Japanese manufacture. One is an Arado AR–196–A–1 from the German battle cruiser *Prince Eugen* which was saved before the ship left Philadelphia for the Bikini Atoll atomic bomb tests after World War II. Actually, two aircraft were unloaded from the ship but one was lost in the Delaware River.

The Arado is a single-engine float plane which was carried aboard battleships and cruisers for reconnaissance and observation. In addition to the *Prince Eugen*, Arados were carried aboard the *Bismark, Graf Spee, Admiral Scheer,*

Japanese Kiwanishi N1K2–J Model 21 "George" exhibited at Willow Grove is of the type used for Kamikaze attacks on U.S. ships during the latter part of World War II. (Courtesy of the U.S. Navy.)

Scharnhorst and other capital ships. The one at Willow Grove is known to have operated in the North Sea and North Atlantic where the *Prince Eugen* accounted for the sinking of more than half a million tons of Allied shipping.

A second German aircraft on display is a Messerschmitt ME–262–Bla Sturmvogel which was brought to Patuxent River Naval Air Station after World War II for evaluation and testing.

The ME–262 was the first jet-powered warplane to engage in combat. Because of its high performance, it might have had a profound effect on the aerial war in Europe if it had been introduced prior to late 1944. The model displayed at Willow Grove is one of only two ME–262s which survived the war.

There are also three Japanese aircraft in the collection; these were also evaluated at Patuxent Naval Air Station after World War II. A Zero was also exhibited until 1965 when it was transferred to the National Air and Space Museum.

One Japanese aircraft which may be seen is a Kawanishi N1K1 Kyofu 11 "Rex" which was used as a floatplane fighter by the Imperial Navy. Only 97 of these were built.

Another aircraft is the Japanese Nakajima B6N1 Tenzan torpedo bomber, known as a Jill 12 to the Allies. It is probably the last existing aircraft of its type.

The third Japanese aircraft is a Kawanishi N1K2–J Model 21 "George" which was originally a fighter aircraft, but which was also used extensively for Kamikaze attacks late in the war. It evolved from a floatplane, the Kawanishi N1K1 Kyofu, which is included in the Willow Grove collection.

Three U.S. Naval aircraft on display are the Chance Vought F7U Cutlass, the North American AF–1E Fury, and the Convair YF2Y–1 Sea Dart. Rounding out the collection is a Lockheed F–80 Shooting Star, the first operational jet fighter aircraft used by U.S. forces, which was introduced in 1946.

Location: Willow Grove Naval Air Station is six miles south of Doylestown, Pennsylvania on Route 611, and some 25 miles north of Philadelphia. There is a small parking area off Route 611 where the aircraft may be viewed.

Schedule: Available during daylight hours.

Admission: Free.

SOUTHEAST

The Alabama Space and Rocket Center is a 35-acre complex. It's the largest collection of rockets, missiles, and spacecraft on permanent exhibit in the United States. It is owned and operated by the Space Science Exhibit Commission of the State of Alabama. (Courtesy of the Alabama Space and Rocket Center.)

Alabama Space and Rocket Center
Huntsville, Alabama

Termed "the best facility of its kind in the world" by Wernher von Braun, who helped to found it, the Alabama Space and Rocket Center is operated as a "living" museum in which visitors can not only touch, but can actually sample experiences similar to those of the astronauts.

The first sight which strikes visitors is that of more than two dozen rockets and missiles of every type standing in a four-acre rocket park. The center even has a simulated moon crater, with a diameter of 100 feet, which contains an Apollo lunar module and two models of astronauts.

The exhibit building, which was opened in March, 1970, contains some 50,000 square feet of display space and offices, as well as a snack bar serving packaged "space food," two information centers, rest rooms, and a 250-seat auditorium.

The interior of the building is divided into 12 areas, with the central one containing full-size space hardware such as actual Mercury and Apollo spacecraft, as well as a mock-up of a Russian Vostok spacecraft. Also on display here are a moon-buggy and Apollo lunar module, along with rocket engines used to power the V–2, Redstone, Saturn, and other rockets. Full-size mock-ups of Surveyor, Lunar Orbiter, Mariner, Syncom, Nimbus, and the Pegasus Meteroid Detection satellite hang overhead.

Close to the entrance is a moon rock display and a National

Aeronautics and Space Administration Visitor Center. A Satellite Tracking Station located here receives and displays weather information directly from space. The Wernher von Braun Recognition Room is nearby, containing many of the awards, honorary degrees, and other honors bestowed on the scientist.

The auditorium is used to show the Center's film, *Freedom to Explore,* which runs for 11 minutes, as well as various NASA films which are scheduled throughout the day.

Visitors to the Space and Rocket Center may also add a guided bus tour of NASA's George C. Marshall Space Flight Center to their visit. The two-hour trip around NASA's 1800-acre complex goes into a number of working areas, including test stands for the Apollo/Saturn V moon rocket, simulators, and mock-ups of future spacecraft under development. These daily tours are subject to schedule variations depending on activity at the Marshall Space Flight Center, which has most recently been involved in the Skylab program.

The Space and Rocket Center covers the development of rocketry and space exploration not only in recent years, but also has one area devoted to rocket pioneers such as Robert H. Goddard, Hermann Oberth, Toftoy, and Wernher von Braun. In the Space Applications area, space suits and equipment used by the astronauts are exhibited and the story of Skylab is illustrated. In addition to the present, the future is projected in a Future in Space section containing models of Skylab, Space Shuttle, Space Station, Space Base, Space Tug, and a Mars Lander, along with an exhibit on the benefits which have been derived from space exploration.

Considerable emphasis is placed on educational exhibits, starting with the models and panels illustrating the solar system. For youngsters, however, much of the enjoyment in visiting the Center lies in the many exhibits equipped with buttons, levers, and switches so that visitors can actually operate the equipment. These include pressing the firing button on a rocket engine which generates five pounds of thrust for ten seconds while the visitor adjusts the control lever. Also included are a heart monitoring system which lets visitors check their own heart rates, and an action-reaction exhibit which contrasts the power of a propellor with that of a

The Alabama Space and Rocket Center has numerous exhibits which youngsters can touch and operate. Emphasis is placed on experiencing the sights and sounds of the space age. (Courtesy of the Alabama Space and Rocket Center.)

rocket engine in a vacuum jar. Visitors can take the controls of the lunar module moon landing simulator to see if they can make a safe landing on the moon with a limited amount of fuel, then they can sit in a Gyro Chair in a simulated spacecraft and feel how a gyroscope stabilizes their position. An Air Chair which rides on a cushion of air has thrusters and other controls for visitors to manipulate. A Mercury capsule has controls which a visitor can handle while sitting in the astronaut's seat. Space scales allow one to check his relative weight on Earth, Mars, and the Moon, and a touch of a hand will bend a beam of light. Two people can play the Preparedness Game, using a missile strategy computer; a missile system can be designed and tested in simulated combat situations.

Center technicians also operate exhibits, such as the Hybrid Rocket Craft, a mockup of a lunar module, which takes off, hovers, and lands on a simulated moon surface.

A singular feature of the Center is that it has never adopted a "don't touch" policy and that it constantly updates and changes exhibits to keep them current. The recommended time to see everything is close to two hours, but there are many things to do as well as see, and families with several children should take this into account.

As one leaves the exhibit building to enter the rocket park, there is a small picnic area.

Hardware displayed in the rocket park includes the Saturn I, a V–1 and V–2, the U.S. Army Jupiter and Juno II, and a Redstone rocket. Also displayed are the Mercury-Redstone, a Mercury–Atlas, a U.S. Air Force Titan and, largest of all, the three stage Apollo Saturn V moon rocket, 363 feet in length.

Other rockets on display include the Lance surface-to-surface missile, Entac, Sergeant, Nike–Hercules, Nike–Ajax, Nike–Zeus, Hawk, Hermes, Corporal, Honest John, Little John, Lacrosse, Pershing, and the U.S. Air Force Hound Dog.

The Alabama Space and Rocket Center is owned and operated by the State of Alabama through its Space Science Exhibit Commission. The entire facility is valued in excess of $20 million. Officials note that visitors have not only come to Tranquility Base from all of the United States, but also from some 76 foreign countries.

Location: Tranquility Base is located on Route 20 just west of Huntsville, 15 minutes from Interstate 65. Huntsville is in northern Alabama, about 100 miles north of Birmingham. Adequate parking is available.

Schedule: 9 a.m. to 5 p.m. from September through May; 9 a.m. to 6 p.m. from June through August. Open every day except Christmas Day.

Admission: Adults $2.00 for the Space and Rocket Center, and $1.35 for the NASA bus tour, with a combination price of $3.00. Children ages 6 to 12, 95 cents for the Space and Rocket Center, and 80 cents for the NASA bus tour, with a combination price of $1.50.

The exhibit building, which includes a 250-seat auditorium has 50,000 square feet of display space. (Courtesy of the Alabama Space and Rocket Center.)

Eight aircraft have been acquired for display in the Battleship
Alabama Memorial Park. The park covers 75 acres of property and
has a 500-car parking lot. (Courtesy of the U.S.S. Alabama
Battleship Commission.)

Battleship Alabama Memorial Park
Mobile, Alabama

It's a bit unusual to visit a small collection of military aircraft and have the opportunity to tour a battleship and a submarine at the same time. Of course, the aircraft collection is secondary as an attraction; however, the *USS Alabama* Battleship Commission considers its 75-acre park site at the head of Mobile Bay a memorial to all military services, and has therefore sought to acquire representative items from each.

The Commission was established as a non-profit agency by the state in 1963. The battleship was donated by the U.S. Navy in 1964 and opened to the public in January of the following year. The submarine, *USS Drum (SS-228)*, is a World War II submarine and it was opened to the public in July, 1969.

The interesting story behind how the battleship came to Mobile developed after the Navy announced plans to scrap it at Bremerton, Washington. The people of Alabama contributed $1,000,000 to save it, and 10 percent of this amount was raised by school children. The vessel was towed from the West Coast to Mobile, some 5600 miles.

For the record, the *Alabama* started her World War II career on escort duty in the North Atlantic, convoying shipping to Murmansk, Russia. At the end of 1943, she joined the Pacific fleet and earned battle stars at the Gilbert Islands, the

Marshall Islands, Hollandia, the Marianas, the Western Carolines, Leyte, Okinawa, and against the Japanese home fleet. She accounted for 22 Japanese aircraft during her six major campaigns. She was present at the surrender ceremonies in Tokyo Bay in 1945.

The *Drum* accounted for 15 enemy ships totaling 84,640 tons during World War II, and earned 12 battle stars.

To make touring easier for visitors, the Commission provides a self-guide folder explaining how to find one's way around aboard the *Alabama*. A series of red, green, and yellow arrows are used to point the direction to follow.

In addition to a gift and souvenir shop for visitors, there is also a picnic area, although there are no facilities available for purchasing snacks or refreshments.

A total of eight aircraft are displayed within the park and near the entrance to the battleship. The two Navy aircraft are an F6F Hellcat and an OS2U Kingfisher scout; a Marine Corps F4U Corsair fighter is also exhibited, as is a Coast Guard HU–16E Albatross rescue amphibian.

Air Force planes include a P–51 Mustang, a B–25 Mitchell, a C–47 Skytrain, and a CH–21B Workhorse helicopter.

Several pieces of Army equipment, including a tank and three field guns, round out the equipment on static display.

Location: The Battleship Alabama Memorial Park is located on Battleship Parkway (routes 31, 90, and 98), five minutes east of downtown Mobile. There is a 500-car parking lot.

Schedule: Open daily from 8 a.m. to sunset. No organized tours are available, but printed tour guides are provided for visitors.

Admission: $2.00 for adults, 50 cents for children under 12 years of age, no charge for children under six. A discount of 25 percent is available for organized groups. Military personnel in uniform are admitted without charge.

U.S. Army Aviation Museum
Fort Rucker
Ozark, Alabama

The U.S. Army Aviation Museum at Fort Rucker, Alabama, tells the story of more than 30 years of Army aviation, not only in terms of the aircraft used, but also through exhibits which highlight achievements, combat use, and technical developments. The museum is noteworthy in that it has the largest collection of helicopters of any museum in the world: fully 40 out of the facility's almost 70 aircraft are rotary wing.

The museum is housed in three World War II buildings with a total of 19,000 square feet of display space. An additional 40,000 square feet of exterior display area is used by the museum to show many of its fixed wing and rotary wing aircraft. In addition to the aircraft on exhibit, the museum also has an outstanding collection of more than 1800 books, documents, manuals, and memorabilia. A photographic collection of pictures related to Army aviation during the past 30 years is used to prepare special exhibits and is available to researchers in military history.

Fort Rucker has been the "home" of Army aviation since 1953. It is also the location of Army aviation pilot training, combat training, maintenance, air traffic control, and aeromedical training. Plans for an aviation museum were first set in 1955 and recognized by the Department of the Army as an integral part of the Army's museum system in 1963. The museum was operated and directed by volunteers for the first

The U.S. Army Aviation Museum contains almost 70 aircraft, including the world's most complete helicopter collection. (Courtesy of the U.S. Army).

several years until a full-time curator was retained in 1966. The museum moved into its present facilities in 1968 and is the official repository for all Army aviation history, trophies, and awards. The Army Aviation Museum Association, Inc. is a non-profit organization which has undertaken fund-raising and operates the museum's souvenir counter to provide private support for the maintenance and future expansion of the museum's facilities.

In addition to its aircraft displays, the museum also has permanent exhibits on the role of Army aviation in Vietnam, a memorial to those who gave their lives in Southeast Asia, a Medal of Honor panel, Army aviation uniforms, and an art gallery.

Exhibits in the museum are laid out in chronological sequence, starting with a prologue about Professor Lowe's observation balloon during the Civil War. The main emphasis is on World War II and later periods, with most of the aircraft being those that saw service in Korea and Vietnam when Army aviation in support of the ground soldier became a vital part of the combat mission.

Among the various helicopters which may be viewed is the Sikorsky R–4B Hoverfly of 1943, the first production model helicopter produced for the U.S. Army and other services. Others include the Bell OH–13B Sioux, Hiller OH–23A Raven, Sikorsky YH–18, McCulloch YH–30, Sikorsky H–19D Chickasaw, Piasecki CH–21 Shawnee, Piasecki H–25A Mule, Sikorsky XH–39, McDonnell XV–1, Hiller YH–32 Hornet, Bell XH–40 Iroquois, Sikorsky CH–34A Choctaw, Sikorsky CH–37B Mojave, Cessna YH–41 Seneca, Brantley YHO–3BR, Bell OH–4A, Fairchild–Hiller OH–5A, Hughes OH–6A Cayuse, Bell AH–1G Huey Cobra, and Bell VCH–34 Choctaw, which is the Executive Flight Detachment version which provided transportation for the President of the United States and other heads of state.

In the role of airborne artillery spotting, a number of fixed wing aircraft served the U.S. Army, starting with the first Piper Cubs which were introduced at the 1941 Louisiana maneuvers. Most of these are well represented in the museum's collection. Among them are the Piper L–4 Grasshopper, Vultee–Stinson L–5 Sentinel, Convair L–13A, Aeronca L–16A Champion, North American Ryan L–17

General Douglas MacArthur's C–121A Constellation Bataan, which served as an airborne command post during the Korean conflict, wears NASA markings. It serves as a backdrop for a U–1A Otter utility tansport. (Courtesy of the U.S. Army.)

Navion, Cessna L–19A Bird Dog, DeHavilland L–20 Beaver, Piper L–21A Super Cub, and YL–24 Courier.

Various experimental one-man helicopters, originally developed in an effort to provide the foot soldier with greater battlefield mobility, or for special applications such as rescue, are also preserved in the museum's collection. They include such craft as the Hiller XROE–1 Rotorcycle, the Curtiss–Wright VZ–7AP Aerial Jeep, Goodyear XAO–3G1 Inflatoplane, and Del Mar DH–lA Whirlymite.

One aircraft of special interest, which is also the largest in the museum, is the Lockheed C–121A *Bataan,* which was used by General Douglas MacArthur as an aerial command post during the Korean War. Between 1966 and 1969, this aircraft was used by the National Aeronautics and Space Administration as an electronic space capsule simulator for testing the tracking stations used in the Gemini and Apollo space flights. It was presented to the museum in 1970.

Two other aircraft of interest which cannot be seen elsewhere in the United States are a Russian MI–4 Hound, a general purpose helicopter used by the Soviet armed forces and in civil configuration; and an L–200A Morava, built in Czechoslovakia in about 1962.

Location: The U.S. Army Aviation Museum is in the southeast part of Fort Rucker, off Route 231 or Route 84 near Ozark, Alabama. It is near the Daleville Gate on Fourth Avenue. Fort Rucker is 94 miles south of Montgomery, Alabama on Route 231. Ample parking space is available.

Schedule: Open Monday through Friday from 9 a.m. to 4 p.m. Open weekends and holidays from 1 p.m. to 5 p.m. Closed on Christmas Day.

Admission: Free.

Complex 26 blockhouse stands at the center of the museum, with a service tower containing a Redstone missile behind it. The exhibit hall nearby contains a V–2 engine, Kettering Bug, Gemini II, and various satellites and weather rockets. (Courtesy of the U.S. Air Force.)

U.S. Air Force Space Museum
Cape Canaveral Air Force Station
Cocoa Beach, Florida

Right in the heart of Cape Canaveral, launching site for U.S. space flights, the Air Force Space Museum portrays the history of rocketry and tells of the exploration of space in the perfect setting.

The museum is situated on two former launch complexes, 26 and 5/6. It was from this spot that the first two manned U.S. space flights were launched, piloted by Astronauts Alan B. Shepard, Jr. and Virgil L. Grissom. The first U.S. satellite, Explorer I, was launched from Pad 26A.

In the spacious outdoor setting, more than 50 rockets and missiles may be viewed. They represent a complete range of the great variety used for scientific and military applications by the National Aeronautics and Space Administration and the Armed Services.

The museum's three buildings are an exhibit hall and two restored blockhouses. The former contains audio-visual displays, a briefing room and the smaller engines, weather satellites, and the Gemini II capsule.

The blockhouses have been authentically restored, with all the consoles and electronic equipment, including an ICBM guidance system, which were in use during launches. Exhibit materials illustrate the history and development of rockets, how they work, and the support provided by the Air Force for both manned and unmanned space exploration programs.

The Air Force Space Museum has almost **80** different outdoor exhibits to inspect, as well as an exhibit hall and blockhouse with restored firing room. (Courtesy of the U.S. Air Force.)

The museum is at Cape Canaveral Air Force Station, which is station number one in the 10,000-mile Eastern Test Range tracking network which extends into the Indian Ocean. Other tracking stations are in the West Indies, on Ascension Island in the South Atlantic, and in South Africa.

Public parking is located between the two outdoor display areas. Not only are missiles and rockets exhibited, but various pieces of support equipment stand on the two complexes. These include trucks for carrying fuel and liquid oxygen, a transporter truck, telemetry antenna and camera mountings, a rocket sled and tracking radar, fire truck and rescue vehicle, all of which have seen service in support of Cape Canaveral launches and training programs for U.S. astronauts.

Complex 26 is the largest area and contains most of the missilry. The museum provides a printed guide for visitors with an identification key showing each missile and rocket. Touring the area from the main entrance, one can see an Atlas B, Mace A, Aerobee, Navaho, Titan I, the X–24A lifting vehicle, a Thor IRBM, an Agena B, Thor Delta, Lacrosse, Honest John, Little John, Pershing, Sparrow I and III, and Hound Dog A, as well as a German V–1 and the intercontinental range Minuteman I.

Others in the complex include the Skybolt, Rascal, Firebee Drone, Snark, Atlas E, Jupiter, Polaris A–3 and A–1, the Corporal, Nike-Ajax, Tiamat, Bomarc A, Hawk, Subroc, Redstone, Agena A, and Matador.

On the two pads at Complex 5/6 are an erect Jupiter C/W Explorer and a Mercury Redstone, along with most of the support equipment at the museum.

West of Cape Canaveral lies Merritt Island and the Kennedy Space Center (NASA), which has its own visitor center. Commercial bus tours are operated every day starting at 8 a.m. by the contractor which operates the Center for NASA.

Location: The U.S. Air Force Space Museum stands on Complexes 26 and 5/6 at Cape Canaveral Air Force Station, just north of the town of Cocoa Beach. It can be reached on Route A-1-A via the South Gate.

Schedule: Open every Sunday from 9 a.m. to 3 p.m. for visitors in private automobiles. May be viewed daily during guided tours of the Kennedy Space Center by bus.

Admission: Free.

This full-scale 228-foot-long mock-up of the Boeing supersonic transport was transported from Seattle to Florida. It is now the main attraction at the SST Aviation Exhibit Center. (Courtesy of the SST Aviation Exhibit Center.)

SST Aviation Exhibit Center
Kissimmee, Florida

The major attraction at the SST Aviation Exhibit Center in central Florida is a plane which was never built. However, an impressive aircraft and aviation history display has been assembled in a relatively short time around the 288-foot full-scale mockup which was acquired from the Boeing Company in 1972.

The Boeing mock-up was auctioned off less than a year after funds for further development of a U.S. supersonic transport were cut off by Congress. Close to a billion dollars had been spent on development of the aircraft up to that point, $11 million of it on the full-scale aluminum mock-up. It was sold for $31,000.

The winning bid for the mockup was tendered by Marks O. Morrison of Lyman, Nebraska, and Don Otis of Rocklin, California, without any immediate idea of what they might do with the craft. They were convinced, however, that a way must be found to preserve the result of the advanced design and engineering work which had so impressed them upon seeing it in the Boeing hangar.

In February, 1972, they decided to establish a non-profit museum to exhibit the mockup "not as a curiosity, but as an educational facility." The location in Kissimmee, Florida was selected because of its vacation orientation. Close to the Florida Turnpike, it is between Cape Canaveral and Walt Disney World.

It took nine railway cars to move the mock-up from Seattle to Florida. Two former Boeing Company employees supervised the move, assisted by 14 students from the aviation department at South Seattle Community College, and they subsequently reassembled the mockup in its new home.

Along with the mock-up itself, the Center also acquired design drawings, technical data, and various additional components for use in related displays which tell the story of supersonic flight and the 14 years of planning which went into development of the aircraft.

In addition to the SST mock-up, the Center has added several aircraft from various periods. Two World War I German pursuit planes, a Fokker D–VII and a Fokker Triplane, are inside the building, as is a D–18 Beechcraft. Probably the best known aircraft in the group is the *Greater Rockford,* in which an attempt to fly from Rockford, Illinois to Stockholm, Sweden was made in 1928. The pilots ran into heavy winds over Greenland, however, and landed on the icecap there only 24 hours after leaving Rockford. Although the pilots reached safety, the Stinson Detroiter they abandoned remained on the icecap for 40 years until it was recovered in 1968.

Outside the museum building, the aircraft displayed include a B–25 once owned by Howard Hughes, and a Sea Dart, one of only three such water-based jet aircraft produced for the U.S. Navy during the Korean War. It was the first seaplane with jet power, as well as the first seaplane with supersonic capability. Also shown is a Grumman HU–16B Albatross air-sea rescue amphibian, one of the last two operated by the U.S. Air Force until they were retired to museums in 1973.

One interesting display inside the 300- by 80-foot building is the Ted Pulsifer collection of almost 600 aircraft models depicting the development of powered flight over a period of 70 years. For a number of years, the collection was part of a traveling exhibit sponsored by the U.S. Air Force.

Almost as long as the SST mockup is a mural painting by Joann Thrasher, depicting the *Panorama of Flight* through the ages.

Other exhibits include the MA-I Mercury space capsule, Snark, and Matador missiles (on loan from the U.S. Air

One of several aircraft displayed outside the SST Aviation Exhibit Center is the Sea Dart, of which only three were built. (Courtesy of the SST Aviation Exhibit Center.

Force), and the world's most powerful jet engine, designed for use in the supersonic transport. This engine weighs over 23,000 pounds and develops a thrust of 65,000 pounds.

The SST Exhibit Center stands on an 11-acre site. Director of Development Dale D. Reed anticipates that an additional building will be added to the present 24,000-square-foot facility and that additional displays will be acquired.

Location: The SST Aviation Exhibit Center is located at the junction of the Florida Turnpike (Sunshine State Parkway) and Highway 192–441. Kissimmee is 12 miles east of Disney World. There is plenty of free parking.

Schedule: Seven days a week from 10 a.m. until dark. Closed Christmas Day.

Admission: $2.00 for adults; $1.00 for children under 12; children under 6 free. The family plan for two adults and three or more children is $7.00. A twelve-month pass is $4.00. Special group rates for adults at $1.00 per person, for children at 50 cents per person. There is a discount of 50 percent for military personnel in uniform. Civil Air Patrol personnel and Scouts in uniform are admitted free.

A full-scale lunar module is one of several launch vehicles and manned spacecraft on static display outside the visitor information center at Kennedy Space Center. (Courtesy of NASA.)

Kennedy Space Center
Merritt Island, Florida

The start of every journey by U.S. astronauts into space has attracted millions of television viewers, so it is not surprising that the launching site from which their voyages began should be one of the nation's most popular attractions. Since the National Aeronautics and Space Administration opened its visitor center at the John F. Kennedy Space Center in August, 1967, some eight million people have visited the complex.

Escorted bus tours of the Merritt Island facility actually started in 1966 and are still an important part of a visit to the Center. Because points of interest are so widely dispersed, the bus tour covers some 50 miles, stopping at launching pads, NASA's vehicle assembly building, and the mission control center. Several camera stops are made along the way to enable visitors to photograph launch vehicles on their pads.

At the visitor information center, films and lectures are held every day, and numerous manned spacecraft, weather and communications satellites, and other hardware items are on display. The center's exhibits, like those of other NASA facilities, are strongly educational. There is less display of hardware for its own sake, and more descriptive and illustrative material, cutaways, photographs, paintings, and demonstrations. Just about every time NASA has observed a visitor milestone, a family with several children has been honored; it's a highly popular attraction for children and there are times when they come close to outnumbering adult visitors.

Examples of all U.S. manned spacecraft may be seen, from Mercury and Gemini to Apollo, both command module and lunar module. The actual Gemini IX spacecraft is the one used by Astronauts Thomas P. Stafford and Eugene A. Cernan. Also on display is a one-tenth scale model of the Saturn V launch vehicle in which fuel tanks, pumps, engines, and control systems are exposed.

The visitor center has parking for several hundred automobiles, and there is a snack bar and gift and souvenir shop in the building. There are even kennel facilities available at the east end of the building.

The two hour bus tours operate throughout the day and cover the Space Center's industrial area and Launch Complex 39 from which the Apollo and Skylab launches were made. A stop is also made at the U.S. Air Force Space Museum at Cape Kennedy Air Force Station.

The John F. Kennedy Space Center is operated by NASA, with the visitor program conducted by Trans World Airlines under a contract; the bus tours are subcontracted to Greyhound which currently uses about 20 buses to handle the large number of visitors.

The Center is also a national wildlife refuge, and there are 200 different types of birds inhabiting the area. Several endangered species which may be seen include the brown pelican, southern bald eagle, and dusky seaside sparrow.

With visitor counts increasing each year, plans have been formulated to expand the visitor center in several steps. Two additional halls will be added which will more than double the floor space.

Location: The entrance to the Kennedy Space Center is on Route 1, two miles south of Titusville, Florida and may be reached over the Indian River causeway east of Route 1. Parking is available. Private automobiles may drive through the Space Center only on Sundays from 9 a.m. to 3 p.m.

Schedule: The visitor information center is open daily from 8 a.m. until 6:30 p.m. from June 1 until September 10; hours are 8:30 a.m. until 3:30 p.m. from September 11 through May 31. The center is closed on Christmas Day.

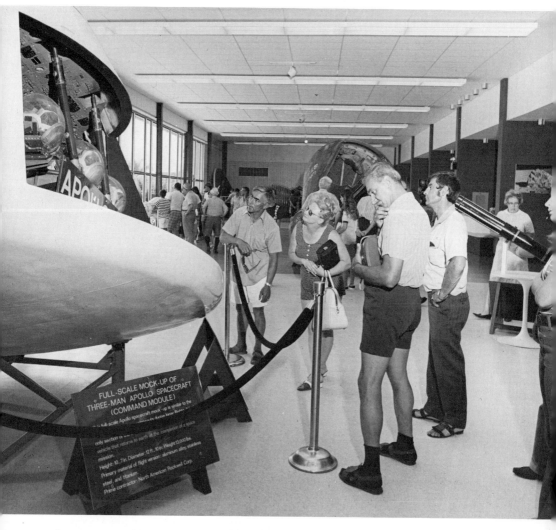

As many as 14,000 visitors a day have toured the Kennedy Space Center, with over eight million visitors recorded since the Center opened in 1967. Actual Mercury, Gemini, and Apollo spacecraft are displayed. (Courtesy of NASA.)

Admission: Free except for the bus tours, which are $2.50 for adults; $1.25 for ages 12 to 18; and 50 cents for children ages three to 11 accompanied by an adult. Active-duty military personnel pay $1.25. Special rates are available for groups.

Reproduction of the Curtiss A–1, which was the first aircraft purchased by the U.S. Navy, and in which Glenn H. Curtiss taught Lieutenant Theodore G. Ellyson to fly. (Courtesy of the U.S. Navy.)

Naval Aviation Museum
Pensacola, Florida

Plans to preserve the heritage of U.S. Naval aviation in a permanent facility were first realized in 1961 when an 8500-square-foot building at Pensacola Naval Air Station was made available as a museum.

The acquisition of historic aircraft, artifacts, and memorabilia greatly exceeded expectations, so that, within a few years, the museum had far more in storage than it could conveniently exhibit to the public. By the end of 1973, when eight aircraft were on display, an additional twenty-nine aircraft were in storage awaiting completion of new facilities.

Soon after the opening of the original building, the need for a permanent building had already become urgent. In 1966, the Naval Aviation Museum Association was formed and incorporated as a non-profit institution, largely through the efforts of the late Admiral Arthur W. Radford, former chairman of the Joint Chiefs of Staff. Admiral Radford had served aboard the battleship *USS South Carolina* in World War I, but earned his wings as a naval aviator in 1920, serving in World War II as commander of Carrier Divisions 11 and 6 in the Pacific Fleet.

The objective of the Association was to raise sufficient funds to construct a permanent museum facility which could be presented to the U.S. Navy to operate and maintain without using public funds.

This portion of the Naval Aviation Museum pays tribute to Navy and Marine Corps aviators who have been awarded the Congressional Medal of Honor. Plaques list the names of organizations and individuals who have contributed to the museum's building fund. (Courtesy of the U.S. Navy.)

Architect Paul K.Y. Chen designed a structure with inherent growth potential which can ultimately be expanded to some 125,000 square feet. Ground was broken for the first stage in November, 1972. The $1.5 million building, with some 60,000 square feet of display area, will open to the public on April 13, 1975.

Like other military museums, the Naval Aviation Museum contains exhibits of not only aircraft, but also of the development of this branch of the Naval service, the conflicts in which men and aircraft have served, and the honors which they have earned.

Tribute is paid to Marine and Naval aviators, numbering a score who have been awarded the Congressional Medal of Honor; also, portraits of all 155 Marine and Naval Aviation prisoners-of-war repatriated from North Vietnam are exhibited.

One exhibit is devoted to the heroism of Torpedo Squadron 8 which attacked the Japanese fleet at the Battle of Midway without benefit of fighter support. Only one aircraft survived; but by the end of the four-day battle the enemy had lost four aircraft carriers and 375 aircraft in a major turning point in the Pacific war.

Other displays include a clear plastic model of an *Essex*-class carrier, carrying scale model aircraft so that visitors can see its inner construction and operation. The development of aviation in the Navy and feats such as the NC–4 aircraft flight across the Atlantic are illustrated with back-lighted panels, photographs, and memorabilia.

The oldest aircraft in the museum is a replica of the Navy's first aircraft, a Curtiss A–1 which was purchased in 1911. The Triad cost $5000 at the time and early naval aviators such as Ellyson, Towers, Cunningham, and Smith had their first flights in it.

Other aircraft included in the museum's comprehensive collection include a Boeing F4B–4, the only specimen in existence of this fighter from the 1920s; a Grumman F6F–5 Hellcat, carrying the markings of the Navy's top ace of World War II, Commander Dave McCampbell; and the only Grumman FF–1 of the mid-1930s known to exist. Also included are a Burgess N–9H World War I seaplane trainer, a Stearman N2S-4 Yellow Peril trainer of World War II, an

RC–45J Expeditor, and a TS–2A Tracker.

Others include a Douglas A–1H Skyraider, a Martin AM–1 Mauler, a Douglas C–47J Skytrain, a Douglas D–558–1 Skystreak, a Lockheed EC–121K Constellation, a McDonnell F2D Banshee, a North American F–1E Fury, a Chance–Vought F4U–5N Corsair, a Douglas F–6A Skyray, a Chance–Vought F–8A Crusader, a Grumman F8F–2 Bearcat, a Grumman F9F–2 Panther, a Grumman TF–11A Tiger, a North American FJ–1 Fury, and a Grumman HU–16D Albatross.

Also on view are a Columbia J2F–6 Duck, a Naval Aircraft Factory MF–Boat, a Naval Aircraft Factory M3N–3 Yellow Peril, a Vought OS2U–3 Kingfisher, a Consolidated PBY–5 Catalina, a Douglas SBD Dauntless, a North American SNJ–5B Texan, a Martin SP–5B Marlin, a Culver TD2C–1, a General Motors TBM–3E Avenger, and a Douglas XF3D Skynight.

The collection's 11 helicopters include Piasecki HRP–1 and HRP–2 Flying Bananas, a Sikorsky H03S–2, a Bell TH–13M Sioux, a Sikorsky CH–19E Chikasaw, a Piasecki, UH–25C Retriever, a Sikorsky UH–34D Seahorse, a Kaman OH–43D, and a Gyrodyne YRON–1.

The space age is not overlooked in the museum, with a number of exhibits featuring Navy pilots who have become astronauts.

Included are Astronaut Scott Carpenter's Mercury capsule, *Aurora 7* and the command module for the Skylab crew composed of Astronauts Conrad, Kerwin, and Weitz, all Navy men.

Location: The Naval Aviation Museum is at the U.S. Naval Air Station, directly south of Pensacola, Florida. From the city, Route 292 leads to Barrancas Avenue which becomes Army Road as it enters the air station. The museum is identified by signs, and adequate parking facilities are available.

Schedule: 8:30 a.m. to 4:30 p.m. Tuesdays through Saturdays, 12:30 to 4:30 p.m. on Sundays. Closed Thanksgiving Day, Christmas Day, and New Year's Day.

Admission: Free.

U.S. Air Force Armament Museum
Valparaiso, Florida

Originally designated as a bombing and gunnery base when it was first activated in 1935, Eglin Air Force Base was destined to become the site for all non-nuclear Air Force weapons testing. For almost two decades, starting at the beginning of World War II, it was known as the Air Proving Ground. Today, it is headquarters for the U.S. Air Force's Armament Laboratory and Armament Development and Test Center.

The idea of establishing an armament museum at the base originated in 1969. Three years later, an agreement with the Okaloosa County Board of Commissioners was reached which calls for the County to operate and maintain the museum while the Air Force provides staff, land, and the building. The base's former service club was set aside to house the museum, and the County appropriated an initial expenditure of $42,000.

The Museum's first director, Lieutenant Colonel William R. Lounsbery, was named in May, 1973, and renovation of the building and collection of display material started.

The Museum was officially opened to the public in June, 1974, with its purpose being to collect, preserve, restore, and display significant and historic items of aircraft armament. The role of Eglin Air Force Base in weapons development during the past thirty years receives particular emphasis.

In addition to specific armament exhibits, the Museum also presents a pictorial history of the U.S. Army Air Corps and the U.S. Air Force from the Wright Brothers' era to the present day, as well as combat photographs from World WarI to Vietnam. Included is a gallery of portraits of all Air Force men who have been awarded the Medal of Honor, the nation's highest decoration.

Some dozen aircraft and missiles are exhibited outside the museum building. These include the P–80 Shooting Star, F–84F Thunderstreak, F–100 Super Sabrejet, F–101 Voodoo, F–102 Delta Dagger, and the F–104 Starfighter. A B–17 Flying Fortress, P–51 Mustang, and F–86 Sabrejet, as well as a Bomarc air-to-air interceptor missile and a Mace ground-to-ground missile can also be seen.

Some 6000 square feet of display area are available inside the building to house the several hundred items on display. These range from aircraft machine guns and cannon dating from World War I to the present, including the GAU–8 30mm aircraft cannon used on the modern A10 aircraft. More than 100 rockets, guided missiles, bombs, and electro-optical guided "smart" bombs are exhibited, along with a German V–1 "Buzz" bomb developed for use against Britain late in World War II.

A number of the ordnance items to be seen are of French, British, German, Japanese, and Russian origin. Rounding out the exhibits are various U.S. aircrew uniforms of wartime periods and a selection of canvases from the U.S. Air Force art collection depicting battle scenes.

Of related interest to visitors to the Valparaiso area is another display, that of the last Air Force B–25, which stands in a park in the town. During World War II, Eglin Air Force Base served as the training site for General James Doolittle and his Tokyo Raid crews. The Doolittle Raiders Memorial honors those men who participated in the attack on the Japanese home islands in April, 1942.

Location: The Air Force Armament Museum is located in Building 871 at Eglin AFB, Florida. It is near the east gate to the base, with ample free parking available. The base can be reached on Route 85 which runs east-west between Valparaiso and Fort Walton Beach, Florida.

Schedule: From 9 a.m. to 4:30 p.m. Tuesday through

Combat scenes and historical photographs are interspersed with rockets, missiles, aircraft bombs of various sizes, and dozens of air-to-air weapons in the Air Force Armament Museum. (Courtesy of the U.S. Air Force.)

Fighter aircraft such as the F–104, F–100, and F–101 are displayed outside the main entrance to the U.S. Air Force Armament Museum at Elgin Air Force Base, Florida. (Courtesy of the U.S. Air Force.)

Saturday; 12:30 p.m. to 4:30 p.m. on Sunday. Closed on Easter Sunday, Thanksgiving Day, Christmas Day, and New Year's Day.

Admission: Free.

Wright Memorial Shaft was erected at Kitty Hawk in 1932. Made of North Carolina granite, it stands 60 feet high atop Kill Devil Hill. (Courtesy of the U.S. Department of the Interior.)

Wright Brothers National Memorial Kitty Hawk, North Carolina

To anyone with a serious interest in aviation, a visit to the place where it all began on a raw December morning in 1903 is a memorable experience. The National Park Service has set aside more than 430 acres at the Wright Brothers National Memorial, with some 2000 square feet of display space in a modern visitor center building which was dedicated in 1960.

Within the visitor center there is a full-scale reproduction of the 1903 Wright Flyer and the 1902 glider used by the Wright brothers. Before their first attempt at *powered* flight on December 17, 1903, the brothers had made more than 1000 flights from the top of Kill Devil Hill between 1900 and 1902. Today, the Wright Memorial Shaft stands atop the hill; a 60-foot pylon of North Carolina granite which was completed in 1932 and is readily visible from the nearby highway.

The visitors center contains several dioramas of the first flight and the preparations which preceded it, as well as a number of exhibits about the brothers themselves, the Kitty Hawk area, and the early wind tunnel experiments conducted by Orville and Wilbur Wright in their bicycle shop in Dayton, Ohio. A number of their original tools and parts of engines, original papers, and personal memorabilia are exhibited in display cases. Upon entering the visitors center, one sees a gallery of oil paintings of several of the aviation pioneers who followed the Wright Brothers in the early years of the century.

The visitors center has an excellent selection of books, as well as airplane models, gifts, and souvenirs for sale. The entire facility is operated by the National Park Service of the U.S. Department of the Interior and it lies within the Cape Hatteras National Seashore.

Between Kill Devil Hill and the visitors center are two wooden buildings, reconstructions of the living quarters and the hangar and workshop used by the Wright brothers. Constructed in 1963, they are furnished with items which duplicate those used by the Wright brothers during their long stays at Kitty Hawk. The area had been suggested to them by the U.S. Weather Bureau in 1900 because of the strong, steady winds which are found there and because it was free of trees and vegetation for miles around.

Near one of the buildings a stone marker indicates the spot from which the brothers commenced the four flights they made on December 17, 1903. A portion of the wooden rail used to guide the aircraft prior to take-off runs lies in a north-south direction beside the granite boulder.

Four numbered markers north of the boulder show the landing points of the first four powered flights. The first three flights were made during the morning and were considerably shorter than the final flight of the day, and this is readily apparent when one views the markers.

The first flight at 10:35 a.m. was piloted by Orville Wright into an irregular gusty wind. In 12 seconds, he covered 120 feet, reached an altitude of 10 feet, and achieved an airspeed of 30 miles per hour. It was during this flight that John T. Daniels took the famous photograph which has been published innumerable times and has been used for murals, dioramas, and illustrations connected with flight in the more than 70 years since.

The second flight at 11:20 a.m. was flown by Wilbur Wright. He covered about 175 feet in 12 seconds. Orville Wright made the third flight at 11:40 a.m. and covered 200 feet in 15 seconds.

It was the fourth flight of the day which undoubtedly impressed the little band of onlookers the most, lasting almost a full minute. As the marker north of the wooden track indicates, it covered a distance of 852 feet in 59 seconds. Unfortunately, a gust of wind later in the day turned the plane

Full-scale replica of the Wright Brothers' first aircraft occupies the gallery at Kitty Hawk visitors center. The original aircraft is displayed in the National Air and Space Museum. (Photo by Jon Allen.)

Granite boulder marks the spot where the Wright Brothers' first flight left the ground. The nearby visitor center contains 2000 square feet of display space with exhibits including full-scale reproductions of 1902 gliders and 1903 aircraft. (Photo by Jon Allen.)

over several times and damaged it badly. In fact, it was never flown again.

The brothers built their second airplane the following year and made more than 100 flights in it at Dayton, Ohio. By 1905, their third plane could remain aloft for more than 38 minutes and make a flight of 24.2 miles. The air age was born. The brothers made many demonstration flights in the years that followed, not only in the U.S., but in France and Germany as well. Wilbur Wright died in 1912 of typhoid fever; Orville lived until 1948.

A visit to the Wright Brothers National Memorial in mid-winter evokes a feeling of the loneliness of the site and the constant winds help capture the feeling of that Thursday morning in 1903. The Memorial Shaft is frequently shrouded in fog and the numerous summer homes between Kill Devil Hill and Kitty Hawk are empty.

While a visitor may be justly impressed by the complex hardware required for space flight, he cannot help but be moved by the lonely, almost secretive, efforts of these two remarkable young brothers. Without help or any support whatsoever they proved, one raw December morning among the deserted dunes at Kill Devil Hill, that man was capable of powered flight.

Location: The Wright Brothers National Memorial is at Kill Devil Hill, 50 miles from Elizabeth City, North Carolina via Route 158. The 431-acre site is 10 miles north of the Cape Hatteras National Seashore, and has a 3000-foot paved airstrip open to private aircraft.

Schedule: Daily, 8:30 a.m. to 4:30 p.m. from November 1 through April 30; 8 a.m. to 6 p.m. from May 1 through October 31.

Admission: Free.

Missiles displayed at the Florence Air and Missile Museum include Bomarc, Titan I, Regulus, Sparrow, Matador, Honest John, and Entac. Even a 22-ton Sherman tank was contributed in 1969. (Photo by Tom Kirkland.)

Florence Air and Missile Museum
Florence, South Carolina

The Florence Air and Missile Museum was conceived in 1963 through the initiative of the local Chamber of Commerce, though its administration subsequently became a joint project of the city and county governments. The land for its establishment at Florence Municipal Airport was contributed by the city.

One of the special features of the outdoor museum, in the words of Thomas C. Griffin, who has served as director since its founding, is "for visitors to be able to touch . . . to enter . . . to become pilot or co-pilot . . . navigator or radio man for even a moment makes all kinds of dreams come true. An imagination is all it takes for a youngster to become a man, and a child's imagination is a marvelous thing." The museum acquired its first aircraft in 1965. When the RB–66–B from Shaw Air Force Base, S.C., an F–86 from McGuire Air Force Base, N.J., and an T–33 from Langley Air Force Base, Va. arrived it was open for business, and even with a small collection, as many as 2500 visitors were recorded over a weekend.

In its first 10 years, the museum has grown to include more than two dozen aircraft and missiles, and claims to be the only museum of its type in the southeast United States and the second largest in the country. A building is being added to the site and will house exhibits on aviation history, engines, and artifacts.

Founded in 1964, the Florence Air and Missile Museum is one of South Carolina's leading tourist attractions. Aircraft on static display include fighters, helicopters, transports, bombers, rescue aircraft, and reconaissance aircraft. (Photo by Tom Kirkland.)

Credit for acquiring many of the aircraft goes to two South Carolina legislators, Senator J. Strom Thurmond and Congressman John L. McMillan, as well as to several military officers who are either natives of the state or who have been stationed at installations there in the last several years.

Aircraft and missiles on display come from locations throughout the country, including military bases in Florida, Ohio, Wisconsin, California, Virginia, Alabama, Kentucky, and Arizona. Several were flown into the Florence airport and demilitarized, while others arrived by truck, and larger missiles were transported by train.

Aircraft in the collection include (in addition to the F–86, RB–66–B, and T–33), a C–119C Flying Boxcar, an HU-16B Albatross air-sea rescue plane, an RB–57–A, a C–97 cargo plane, an F–89–J Scorpion, a WB–47–B, an A–26, an H–21 helicopter formerly used at the White House, an HH–43A helicopter, a C–124 Globemaster, an OH–23 helicopter, a TH–13–M helicopter, and a TF–101–F Voodoo. A B–29 is the latest addition to the aircraft section.

The missiles which may be seen are a Bomarc, a Titan intercontinental ballistic missile, a Regulus, a Sparrow, a Matador, an Entac, and two Honest Johns.

Location: The Florence Air and Missile Museum is located on U.S. Route 301 at the entrance to the Florence Municipal Airport, just east of the city limits. Florence is in the northeast part of South Carolina, 117 miles from Wilmington, North Carolina.

Schedule: Open year-round during daylight hours.

Admission: 50 cents for adults; 25 cents for children under 12 years of age.

Sunday afternoon visitors cluster around Sopwith Pup as the World War I era lives again at the Flying Circus Aerodrome. (Photo by Lou Davis.)

Flying Circus Aerodrome
Bealeton, Virginia

For a heady dose of nostalgia, take a Sunday afternoon drive through the rolling Virginia countryside to Bealeton and the Flying Circus Aerodrome.

Here, from May through October, a dedicated group of men relive the "golden years of flight" with mock World War I dogfights, aerobatics, balloon busting and ribbon cutting, races, and formation flying. There are also comedy acts, sailplane demonstrations, and parachute jumping.

It all started in the summer of 1970 when a diverse group of antique aircraft enthusiasts got together. Some were airline pilots who enjoyed "stick and rudder" flying when off duty, but the group also included a minister, radio commentator, editor, salesmen, architects, and businessmen. They realized that while today's youngsters may see vintage aircraft in museums, there was no way they could experience the sounds and smell and see and touch well-preserved relics of the biplane era.

The original 16 founders of Flying Circus Airshows put up their own money to acquire a Nieuport 24 and tri-wing Fokker Dr–1, then a Sopwith Camel, two German Rumplers, and a DeHavilland BE2C. What had started as a casual endeavor soon become a major weekend attraction with crowds of up to 2000 on hand for their flying programs.

Today, the group has close to thirty board members, all of

whom are stockholders and all of whom participate in the program. In 1973, the 203-acre site 14 miles from Warrenton, Va. at which they had started shows in May, 1971, was finally purchased. Hangars and buildings of the type used in World War I were constructed and a 2000-foot grass runway area was cleared.

Members of their families and friends help out with ground chores and the organization has a full-time caretaker on the field. Since the gates open on Sundays at 10 a.m., visitors are invited to bring picnic luncheons or purchase refreshments at the refreshment building; souvenirs are available there as well as at a counter in the main hangar. For campers, the Deerfield Campgrounds are adjacent to the Flying Circus Aerodrome.

The first half of the Sunday afternoon show features precision flying and a hot air balloon ascension, along with humorous skits provided by "Snoopy" and a harmless "German prisoner" who "steals" a handy aircraft. The second hour is punctuated with wailing sirens, bombs, and "anti-aircraft" fireworks, accompanied by a fighter "scramble" and mock dogfight.

On rain days, of which there are about three each season, and before the air shows, visitors may see the Flying Circus' aircraft in their hangars and scan the growing collection of memorabilia in the "operations" room.

As one member of the group points out, those involved in the Flying Circus have had to revise their opinion of World War I aviators. Just flying the "flimsy crates" was quite an achievement without the added combat role. He adds: "They were truly courageous and talented men whose survival needed large helpings of luck."

In addition to the authentic World War I aircraft which the Flying Circus members have flown since their first show in 1971, other aircraft which participate regularly include four Stearman biplanes, a Waco UPF7, two Fleet biplanes, a Corby Baby Ace monoplane, two Taylorcraft, and a Sopwith Pup.

Visitors to the aerodrome can fly too, with members of the organization offering old-fashioned barnstormer flights at $10 each. Those with a yen for added excitement can make an aerobatic flight for $25.

Flags of nations which fought in World War I fly above the Flying Circus' hangar. Great names of early aviation such as Curtiss, Fokker, Spad, and Sopwith appear on the building. (Photo by Jon Allen.)

Road sign directs visitors to Flying Circus. Sunday afternoon air shows start at 2:30 p.m. (Photo by Jon Allen.)

Since the first Sunday in 1971 when the Flying Circus opened its gates, an estimated 100,000 people have enjoyed its recreation of the "golden years of flight." The show has become highly professional and, as members feel, it's a fitting, living complement to the static exhibits which may be seen at the National Air and Space Museum in nearby Washington.

Location: The Flying Circus Aerodrome is on Route 17 between Fredericksburg and Bealeton, Virginia, 14 miles from the latter town. From the Washington area, it can be reached on Routes 29/211 or Route 28. Private pilots landing at Warrenton-Fauquier Airport are picked up by courtesy car; arrangement can be made by telephoning (703) 439-8661 ahead of time or contacting the airport on unicom 122.8 ten minutes out. The airport has a 4100-foot paved runway.

Schedule: Air shows are presented every Sunday afternoon at 2:30 p.m. from Memorial Day through the end of October. About three cancellations due to weather are the seasonal average.

Admission: $2.50 for adults; $1.50 for children under 16 years of age; no charge for children under six. No charge for parking. Special rates for groups. Telephone: (703) 439-8661.

The U.S. Army Transportation Museum contains some dozen helicopters and fixed-wing aircraft in a 15,000-square-foot display park. It is located near the main gate at Fort Eustis, Virginia. (Photo by Jon Allen.)

U.S. Army Transportation Museum
Fort Eustis, Virginia

Every mode of transportation which has been used to support military operations is illustrated at the U.S. Army Transportation Museum at Fort Eustis, Virginia. Sections in the building's 9000 square feet of interior display area are devoted to the Army rail system, water and motor transport, and to aviation. There are even exhibits which contain a dog sled from Greenland and an oxcart from Vietnam.

Large items are exhibited in the 15,000-square-foot display park adjacent to the museum, near the main gate to the base. Here are railway locomotives and cars, vehicles and amphibians, and a total of about a dozen Army helicopters and fixed-wing aircraft. In addition, several experimental air cushion vehicles can be seen.

The museum was first established in 1959 and has been in its present quarters since 1966, with nine display galleries inside the building.

The aviation gallery contains a number of models and aircraft engines, along with panels which describe the development of early combat aircraft. There is a helicopter cockpit in which visitors may sit and view a slide program on the role of helicopters in Army aviation.

The line-up of aircraft in the display park is easily visible upon entering the main gate at Fort Eustis. Helicopters displayed include a Sikorsky H–19D Chickasaw, Bell

Army aviation from World War I to the present day is illustrated in the Transportation Museum. The helicopter cockpit with slide show is popular with young visitors. (Photo by Jon Allen.)

OH–13B Sioux, Hiller OH–23B Raven, Piasecki CH–21C Shawnee, and a Piasecki UH–25A Mule.

Also on display are fixed-wing aircraft such as a Cessna O–1 Bird Dog, a DeHavilland L20A Beaver, and a U–9.

Fort Eustis is the location of the U.S. Army Transportation School and of Felker Army Airfield, the world's first permanent military heliport, dedicated in December, 1954. Among the prominent military and civilian dignitaries present at the dedication was Igor Sikorsky, designer and manufacturer of many of the helicopters used by the U.S. Army.

According to the Army, some 70 aircraft are based at Felker AAF and there are more than 75,000 takeoffs and landings a year at the base.

Several years ago, a U.S. Army Transportation Corps Museum Foundation was established to raise the necessary funds to construct and maintain a permanent facility. Plans call for a building containing 20,000 square feet of display space, some 5000 square feet of covered display area adjacent to the building, and a 100,000-square-foot display park. To be located near the entrance to Fort Eustis, it is expected to open to the public in 1975. With several times the present available space, the new facility will also have an ability to present its collection in more modern settings than is presently possible in the temporary wooden structure.

Location: The U.S. Army Transportation Museum is at Building 301 in Fort Eustis, which is located in the city limits of Newport News, Virginia, one mile from Route 64. There is ample parking space available.

Schedule: Open from 8 a.m. to 5 p.m. from Monday through Friday, and from 1 p.m. to 5 p.m. on weekends and holidays. Guided tours are available for large groups.

Admission: Free.

Hampton's Aerospace Park and Information Center reflects the involvement of local installations in military aviation and the U.S. space program. (Courtesy of the Hampton Aerospace Park.)

Aerospace Park
Hampton, Virginia

Although Hampton, Virginia is known as a city with a rich colonial history, it is also a community which has figured prominently in civil and military aviation and in the nation's space program. Hampton is a community which, with neighboring Newport News, has an abundance of museums and historic sites.

The National Aeronautics and Space Administration's Langley Research Center is located within the city, adjacent to Langley Air Force Base, the oldest active military air base in the United States.

In the early 1960s, the city decided to establish its Aerospace Park in recognition of the contributions made by NASA and the U.S. Air Force in the area to aviation and space development. The park and the Hampton Information Center are administered by the city and the park contains a special "aerospace playground."

The 15-acre park has more than a dozen aircraft, spacecraft, and rockets, maintained in excellent condition. The city's information center has some 3500 square feet of display space under its geodesic dome, much of which is devoted to aviation and space subjects.

For visitors to the community, the information center is a starting point for a self-guided tour of Hampton which includes a dozen attractions, among them the Langley

Visitors to Aerospace Park can inspect aircraft, picnic, and keep children occupied in the "aerospace playground" during warm weather. (Photo by Jon Allen.)

Research Center and Langley Air Force Base.

Aircraft which are on display in the park include a T–33, an F–86 Sabrejet, an F–89 Scorpion, an F–84 Shooting Star, an F–100 Supersabre, an F–101 Voodoo, as well as a CH–21 Shawnee helicopter, and an SV–5 Lifting Body.

Missiles exhibited are a Nike–Ajax, a Polaris A–2, a Nike, Corporal, Little Joe, and Jupiter. There is also a Mercury capsule and a Pageos satellite.

Location: Aerospace Park and the Hampton Information Center are at 413 West Mercury Boulevard, approximately two miles east of Interstate Highway 64. Motorists on Interstate Highway 64 should take Exit 8, then Route 258 north.

Schedule: Exhibits in Aerospace Park can viewed 24 hours a day throughout the year. The Information Center is open from 8 a.m. to 5 p.m. Monday through Friday and from 9 a.m. to 5 p.m. Saturdays and Sundays between Memorial Day and Labor Day. The Center is closed on Christmas Day and New Year's Day.

Admission: Free.

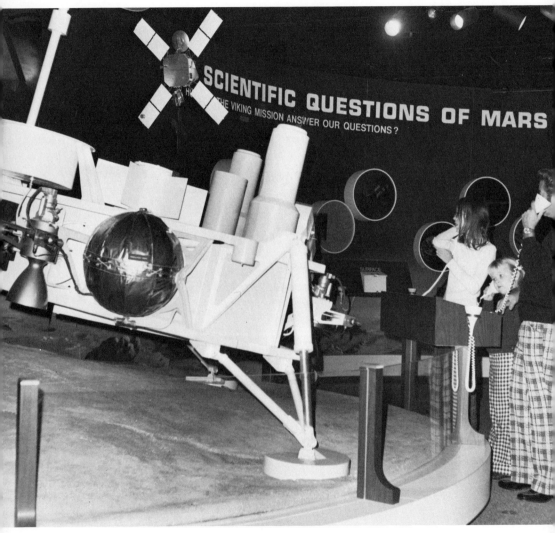

Most exhibits at Langley Research Center, such as the one on the Viking-Mars lander, are equipped with visual and audio educational commentaries. (Photo by Jon Allen.)

Langley Research Center
Hampton, Virginia

The sense of history one feels in Hampton, Virginia extends to the National Aeronautics and Space Administration's Langley Research Center, that organization's oldest facility.

For more than 50 years, the Langley Research Center has conducted aeronautical research, starting with programs on aircraft reliability during World War I. It is also adjacent to Langley Air Force Base, the oldest Air Force installation still in service.

This sense of history contrasts with Langley's modern visitor center, an attractive, fully carpeted 10,000-square-foot building with an array of fascinating exhibits with high appeal to young visitors. During the school year, as many as a dozen class groups tour the Center every day, and there's little rest for the staff on weekends with packs of Cub Scouts awaiting their turn for special film showings and guided tours.

The visitor center is tucked away near the edge of the NASA complex, surrounded by massive buildings which house transonic and hypersonic wind tunnels, space environment facilities, and test beds for rocket engines.

Much of the fascination of the visitor center lies in the fact that very few of the items on display are mockups. The original Apollo XII capsule is on display, along with a sample of lunar rock and Astronaut Alan Shepard's space suit. While the space age receives "stellar" billing, aircraft development and the role of the Langley Research Center are well documented. Most of the exhibits have either visual or audio descriptions to explain their significance.

One section of the Center is devoted to explaining the use of wind tunnels in aircraft design. Several aircraft engines are displayed nearby, and one wall is devoted to the Evolution of Aircraft, using 90 scale models from the Wright Flyer to the Boeing 747. NASA films are shown at regular intervals in the Center's small auditorium which is decorated with large photographs of 20 leading aeronautical personalities. These include the Wright Brothers, Glenn Curtiss, Wiley Post, Amelia Earhart, Lincoln Beachey, Billy Mitchell, and others. A small folder with brief biographical sketches of each of the 20 personalities is available to visitors.

Among the space age exhibits are a mockup of the Viking–Mars Lander, a working weather satellite picture receiving station, a communications satellite, Skylab and space shuttle models, and a lunar orbiter. Each exhibit is in an appropriate setting and an excellent collection of aerospace art illustrates the applications of the mockups and hardware.

Few youngsters can resist getting away from the visitor center without something from the well-stocked souvenir

The visitors center at Langley Research Center has 10,000 square feet devoted to exhibits about the past, present, and future of space flight. (Photo by Jon Allen.)

Astronaut Alan Shepard's space suit is among the numerous items of hardware and equipment on view at Langley Research Center. (Photo by Jon Allen.)

counter. Models, posters, astronaut patches, and numerous other items are available.

According to NASA, research conducted at the Langley Research Center has been applied in some manner to nearly every aircraft and spacecraft that the United States has ever flown. While it has not achieved the fame of other NASA facilities more directly involved in the manned space program, it has played a key role in the program's success. For anyone visiting Hampton, the Center is included on the itinerary of the city tour. While the actual exhibits are most impressive, the Center's unique emphasis on their educational value makes it one of the best-conceived facilities of its type, with a highly effective use of the available space.

Location: NASA's Langley Research Center is on Route 134, north of Hampton, and can be reached via Interstate Highway 64. It's about a 15-minute drive from the city. Upon entering the NASA-Langley Air Force Base gate, directional signs point the way to the Visitor Center. Ample parking is available for cars and buses.

Schedule: The Visitor Center is open daily from 8 a.m. to 4 p.m. and on Sundays from noon until 4 p.m.

Admission: Free. Organized groups should make prior arrangements if special consideration is required.

Aviation Hall occupies most of the second floor in the Marine Corps Museum at Quantico, Virginia, about 30 miles south of Washington, D.C. (Photo by Jon Allen.)

U.S. Marine Corps Museum
Quantico, Virginia

Unless a visitor to the U.S. Marine Corps Museum at Quantico, Virginia climbs the narrow staircase to the second floor, he's likely to miss Aviation Hall. Except for one room which covers Marine Corps participation in the Vietnam conflict, the entire floor is devoted to historical exhibits covering Marine aviation from 1912 to the present day.

Marine Corps aviation dates from 1912, since that is the year in which the first officer was assigned to flight instruction. He was Alfred A. Cunningham, a young man who enlisted at the age of 16 to take part in the Spanish-American War. When he completed his flight training at Annapolis in 1912, he received a rating as Marine Corps aviator no. 1 and Naval aviator no. 5.

A prominent place in Aviation Hall is occupied by the Cunningham Award which was established in his memory in 1960. It is awarded annually to the Marine Corps aviator of the year.

The exhibit areas in the museum cover the development of Marine Corps aviation during its formative years and in two World Wars. Display cases full of memorabilia and documents are interspersed with dioramas showing Marine combat aircraft in action.

The World War I period was an especially interesting one for Marine Corps aviation, with two main operations being conducted. Marine aviators served on the Western Front with the Northern Bombing Group. The First Marine Aviation Force was based at La Fresne, flying DH–4B and DH–9 aircraft. Another Marine aviation unit was stationed on Sao Miguel in the Azores Islands where they operated Curtiss R–6 seaplanes on U-boat patrol during 1917 and 1918.

From a pre-war force of five officers and 18 enlisted men, Marine aviation grew to a strength of 282 officers and 2180 enlisted men by the end of the war. Among the officer ranks there were six future generals whose appreciation of the role of airpower in modern warfare would have a significant influence in the Pacific 25 years later.

During the formative years after World War I, Marine aviators served throughout the world with U.S. military units based in such places as Haiti, Guam, Nicaragua, China, and the Philippines. When General Claire L. Chennault organized the American Volunteer Group (AVG), known as the Flying Tigers, in the late 1930s to fight in China, a number of former Marine aviators were among the first to join his organization.

Marine Corps aviation supported ground units throughout the Pacific campaign in World War II, as well as conducting fighter operations from carriers. One display case in the museum covers this period and features exhibits and memorabilia of the Corps' two leading aces of World War II, Major G.M. Boyington and Captain Joseph J. Foss.

In addition to the museum building itself, a 1920 vintage hangar at Quantico's Brown Field houses 25 aircraft which have been used by the Corps since the beginning of its aviation service.

The hangar houses a shop and offices and is open for tours to the public only through prior arrangements with the public affairs office at Quantico. A number of the combat aircraft in the aviation section are unique and are not known to be in any other museum.

The aircraft include a DH–4 and the only Marine Corps F4F which still exists, as well as the only two F7Fs in a museum.

Also included are an F6F, F8F, F9F, SBD, a Japanese Zero, a Baka bomb, an FH–1, F2H, F4D, FJ–3, F11F, AD–4, AD–5, HRS–3, VH–34, OH–13, YRON–1, X–28A, FG1D, F4U–F, JRF–5, and JD–1.

The oldest plane in the collection, and the one which was not flown by the Marine Corps, is a 1911 Bleriot which was found some years ago in a Massachusetts barn. It is the same type in which the first Marine aviator, Alfred A. Cunningham, learned to fly in 1912.

Plans for expansion of the U.S. Marine Corps Museum, especially the aviation section, were proposed in 1972. When realized, the museum will be able to display its aircraft in an adequate setting, along with engines, equipment and materials, dioramas, and related memorabilia. A 75,000- square-foot interior display area has been recommended.

Location: The U.S. Marine Corps Museum is located next to the main post exchange at the Marine Corps Base at Quantico, Virginia. The base is 31 miles south of Washington, D.C. on Route 95, and about 35 miles north of Fredericksburg, Virginia. Groups may make tour arrangements by writing in advance to the Deputy Director for Marine Corps Museums at Quantico or telephoning (703) 640-2606.

Schedule: Open from 10 a.m. to 5 p.m., Monday through Saturday, and from noon to 5 p.m. on Sundays and holidays.

Admission: Free.

MIDWEST

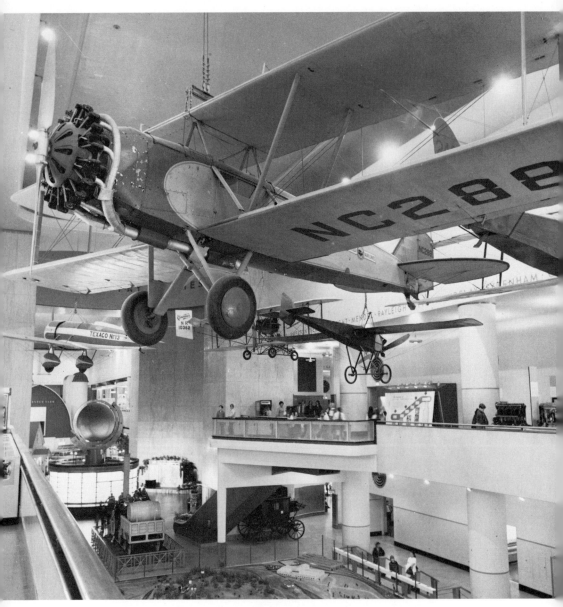

The East Court of the Museum of Science and Industry shows a Boeing 40–B airmail plane operated by United Air Lines in the foreground, and, left to right: the Texaco No. 13 Travelair Speed plane in which Frank Hawks established many speed records, a Curtiss Wright pusher biplane of 1910, and a Morane Saulnier of 1913. (Courtesy of the Museum of Science and Industry.)

Museum of Science and Industry
Chicago, Illinois

The Chicago Museum of Science and Industry contains several interesting aviation and aerospace exhibits, although they are not all situated together.

On the main floor, there are three sections of interest. The first, a display of historic aircraft, is among the sights which first greet visitors at the main entrance.

Also on the main floor is a full-scale passenger cabin of a Boeing 747 jumbo jet. This, like many other individual exhibits in the museum, is sponsored by a corporation (in this case, United Air Lines) and is part of a display telling the story of the growth of commercial aviation.

Beyond the Boeing 747 in the museum's east pavilion there is a National Aeronautics and Space Administration exhibit which contains the actual Apollo VIII spacecraft which made the first manned flight around the moon. Replicas of several space satellites are also part of this display, and films tracing the history of the U.S. space program are shown to visitors.

Close to the center of the east pavilion is a permanent U.S. Air Force exhibit. Its theme is research and development, and the displays cover the fields of communications, weapons, and flight medicine.

The balcony above the museum's main floor also contains a larger exhibit of historic aircraft, as well as two adjacent sections on man in space and aircraft engines.

The aircraft contained in the museum include a Morane Saulnier of 1913, a Curtiss JN–4 Jenny of 1917, a Travelair Speed Plane acquired from Texaco, and a Boeing 40–B airmail monoplane of 1913 acquired from United Air Lines. Also in the collection are two World War II combat aircraft, a British Supermarine Spitfire 1A and a German Junkers 87–B Stuka bomber, both of which were donated to the museum by the British government.

Among the spacecraft, in addition to the Apollo VIII command module, are a Mercury capsule, a Mariner II satellite, a Nimbus weather satellite, a Relay communications satellite, and a Syncom communications satellite.

The engine section contains a total of 18 engines, ranging from a Wright Brothers engine of 1910 and a Gnome of 1916 to more modern Pratt & Whitney, Siddley, Rolls–Royce Merlin Mark III, and Packard engines.

Apollo VIII command module which carried Astronauts Frank Borman, James Lovell, and William Anders ten times around the moon. Colonel Borman's space suit is also part of the museum's space exploration exhibit. (Courtesy of the Museum of Science and Industry.)

With some 14 acres of area divided into 75 exhibit halls, the Chicago Museum of Science and Industry is one of the most comprehensive museums of its type in the world. More than three million visitors pass through it each year. Its building was constructed in 1893 for use as the fine arts building at the Columbian Exposition. It opened in its present form in 1933, largely through the efforts of the late Julius Rosenwald, president and chairman of Sears, Roebuck and Company, a year after his death.

In addition to the aviation and space exhibits, visitors will find numerous other exhibits of interest. A sampling includes halls for communications, photography, automobiles, nuclear science, seapower, a coal mine, computers, medicine, and others.

Location: The Chicago Museum of Science and Industry is in Jackson Park at 57th Street and South Lake Shore Drive. There is plenty of free parking and five bus routes (Nos. 1, 2, 5, 28, and 55) stop at the museum. There is also a railway station two blocks from the museum.

Schedule: Open daily from 9:30 a.m. to 5:30 p.m. Monday through Saturday, and from 10 a.m. to 6 p.m. on Sundays and holidays during the summer. Open daily from 9:30 a.m. to 4 p.m. Monday through Saturday, and from 10 a.m. to 6 p.m. on Sundays and holidays in the winter. Closed on Christmas Day.

Admission: Free.

This Republic P–47M is among two dozen war planes at the Victory Air Museum. The aircraft flew in the 1948 Bendix Trophy Race and has since been restored to the markings of the 78th Fighter Group. (Photo by Earl Reinert.)

One of four Messerschmitt ME–109Gs, built in Spain, bears markings of the Finnish Front, 1940. Victory Air Museum's Messerschmitts were used in filming the movie *Battle of Britain*. (Photo by Earl Reinert.)

Victory Air Museum
Mundelein, Illinois

The emphasis is on World War II and the aircraft are some of the most famous combat aircraft used by the Allies and the Axis at the Victory Air Museum, less than 30 miles from Chicago.

For starters, the museum boasts six Messerschmitt ME–109s— the largest collection of this model in the world.

Toward the end of World War II, aviation historian Earl Reinert assembled various airplane parts and an excellent library at his home in Arlington Heights, Illinois, and within a short time started acquiring surplus combat aircraft. In 1952, following a tour of Pacific battlefields, he resolved to try to preserve as many combat aircraft of the period as possible and create a museum to house them. Now, more than 20 years later, he and his associate, Paul Polidori, have two dozen assorted aircraft, plus various trucks, searchlights, engines, and spare parts. Reinert's excellent library on World War II aviation and his own thorough knowledge of the subject assure a remarkable degree of authenticity in restoring and displaying the collection.

Reinert purchased a Lockheed P–38 and Republic P–47 after the war, sponsoring them in the Bendix Trophy Races of 1947 and 1948 respectively. Both times, aviatrix Jane Page piloted his aircraft.

Because of his ownership of the P–47, Republic Aviation

contacted him in 1950 when they were seeking spare parts for several foreign air forces which still operated Thunderbolts, and he assisted them for several years in this respect. He still has a stock of spare parts, but his own P–47M is no longer in flying condition.

Other U.S. combat aircraft on the field include a North American B–25J Mitchell with Fifth Air Force markings and a Douglas RB–26C Invader, as well as the fuselage and engine of a North American P–51K/F6 Mustang. Former Navy aircraft are a Grumman FM–2 Wildcat with one wing in Navy markings and the other in U.S. Marine Corps markings, and a Grumman F6F–3 Hellcat fuselage and engine. The latter aircraft has a combat history dating from 1944 when Lt. Alex Vraciu shot down five enemy aircraft in it during the Battle of Truk Island. The one flying boat in the collection is a Consolidated PBY–6A Catalina, dating from 1944, which was used as a business airplane briefly after the war.

On the Axis side, the Messerschmitt ME–109 collection is the leading attraction. Actually, ME–109Gs, they were built in Spain between 1959 and 1961 and equipped with Rolls Royce engines, then used in filming the movie *Battle of Britain.* Reinert has assembled four of the aircraft and painted them in various markings, such as the Libyan desert, the Finnish front, and the Russian front. When the remaining two are assembled, he plans to maintain all six in flying condition and operate them from Polidori Airfield, since all have less than 100 hours of flying time on them.

Other aircraft which can be viewed by visitors are a 1938 Lockheed Hudson, operated at one time by Trans Canada Airlines, and painted in the markings of the RAF Coastal Command; a North American T–28A trainer; a North American AT–6 Texan trainer; and a Beech C–45. One of the most unusual items is a Japanese Ohka 11 Baka Bomb 1–13 suicide aircraft, one of six captured in a cave in Okinawa in 1945. Reinert also has a Boeing B–17G Flying Fortress in storage which he expects to move to Polidori Airfield to join the collection on display.

Location: The Victory Air Museum is located at Polidori Airstrip on Gilmer Road, North, three miles west of the town of Mundelein on Route 176. Mundelein and its neighboring town of Libertyville are only 30 miles northwest of Chicago.

Six Messerschmitt ME–109G aircraft are included in the Victory Air Museum collection. Their markings represent various World War II fronts on which the Luftwaffe fought from Africa to the Arctic. (Photo by Jon Allen.)

This Japanese Okha 11 Baka Bomb is one of six captured in an Okinawa cave in 1945. (Photo by Jon Allen.)

There is plenty of free parking. A 2000-foot airstrip is open to private pilots.

Schedule: Open daily except Tuesdays from 9 a.m. to sunset. Fly-bys of some of the aircraft in the museum's collection and others are held on Sunday afternoons.

Admission: $1.00 for adults and 25 cents for children under 12 years of age.

The Airpower Museum is the center of many of the activities of the Antique Airplane Association. Facilities are available for the restoration, repair, and maintenance of vintage aircraft. (Courtesy of the Airpower Museum.)

Airpower Museum
Blakesburg, Iowa

To vintage aircraft enthusiasts, Antique Airfield is the home of the Antique Airplane Association, one of the nation's largest organizations devoted to restoring and preserving vintage aircraft, as well as the site of numerous well-attended fly-ins each year. The organization's annual classic and antique gathering each Labor Day weekend, for instance, brings well over 300 aircraft to Blakesburg from every part of the country.

At the Airpower Museum, which is situated adjacent to the Association's headquarters, emphasis in on the period between World War I and World War II and most of the aircraft which may be seen are in flying condition. The museum is affiliated with the Antique Airplane Association and shares many of the same facilities.

The Airpower Museum currently owns a 30-acre site on which its main display hangar, a storage hangar, caretaker's home, bunkhouse and annex for exhibits, offices, and library are situated. The museum's 15,000 square feet of space includes a book shop and souvenir counter, while there is a restaurant and snack bar at the Antique Aircraft Association section of the airport. During fly-ins and other special occasions, the museum opens its own snack bar for visitors.

The museum was founded as a non-profit organization in 1964 and was first housed in a former Navy training building at the Ottumwa Industrial Airport. Construction of the present facilities started in 1971, to a large degree as the result of the dedicated efforts and organizational ability of the museum's first president, the late J.G. Lowe of Denver, Colorado. Administration of the museum is by an 11-member board of directors. The museum publishes a 12-page quarterly newsletter devoted to museum activities, forthcoming events, individual vintage aircraft, news of other aviation museums, and items available in the APM store.

The museum's display hangar contains more than a dozen aircraft in flying condition, while the storage hangar holds several additional aircraft and portions thereof awaiting restoration.

Aircraft which may be seen include a 1925 Anderson biplane with OX–5 engine, a 1931 Stinson JR–s, a 1930 Monocoupe 90, a 1935 Rearwin Sportster, a 1929 Fairchild 71, a 1940 Ryan PT–22, a 1939 Rearwin Cloudster, a 1931 Stearman 4E, a 1933 Taylor E–2 Cub, a 1937 Arrow Sport F, a 1939 Aeronca LC, a 1937 Aeronca K, and a World War II Culver PQ–14 target airplane.

The museum's particular field of interest spans the 1920s and 1930s, with most of the related exhibits covering these years including the pioneering airmail era. The museum's excellent library contains numerous books autographed by prominent aviators who played roles in the development of aviation during this period.

The museum and its facilities serve as headquarters for the numerous fly-ins held at Antique Airfield. These range from the annual Labor Day weekend event to special occasions when owner-pilots of particular types of aircraft gather to compete, swap yarns, and socialize. Aircraft types such as Rearwins, Fairchilds, Luscombes, World War II trainers, Tiger Moths, and others arrive with proud owners at the controls for two or three days at Antique Airfield, hence the museum's bunkhouse and camping facilities.

Similar events and other fly-ins are held throughout the country by the Antique Airplane Association's state and local chapters, and a calendar of such occasions is published both in the museum bulletin and in the AAA's bi-monthly magazine, *Antique Airplane News.*

Location: The Airpower Museum is located at Antique

Airfield in Blakesburg, about 12 miles west of Ottumwa, Iowa on Route 34.

Schedule: 8 a.m. to 6 p.m. Monday through Saturday and 1 p.m. to 6 p.m. on Sundays. Special arrangements are available for school and tour groups.

Admission: Free; donations customary. There are registration fees for special events held at Antique Airfield.

The Harold Krier Aerobatic Museum occupies a 6700-square-foot addition to the Clark County Historical Society's Pioneer Museum. Located on Route 160 in Ashland, Kansas, it was dedicated in 1974. (Courtesy of *The Clark County Clipper.*)

Harold Krier Aerobatic Museum
Ashland, Kansas

For well over a decade, Harold Krier was the foremost aerobatic pilot in America, winner of every award and trophy offered in this exacting and thrilling sport. His performances in air shows from coast to coast were seen by hundreds of thousands of spectators.

Krier was respected as an individual throughout his career and was ever-popular with audiences. He was held in great esteem by his colleagues and competitors, for he was never too busy to lend a helping hand, nor too successful to remain the unsophisticated ranch boy from Olpe, Kansas, who had left home to enlist in the Air Corps during World War II.

Following his death in an aviation accident in June, 1971, several organizations and individuals formed a non-profit corporation in Kansas to establish the Harold Krier Field Aerobatic Museum in Ashland. It is the only museum of its type in the country and, in fact the only museum anywhere in which so much is devoted to the subject of aerobatics.

The museum is a 6700-square-foot addition to the community's Pioneer Museum, managed by the Clark County Historical Society. Occasional air shows are presented at Harold Krier Field nearby as fundraising events to support and maintain the museum.

Three of the aircraft flown by Krier during his many air show appearances in national and international competitions are owned by the museum. These are his Great Lakes, DeHavilland Chipmunk, and the Krier Kraft-Akromaster.

Krier's trophies and awards, numbering more than 30, are displayed in the museum, along with numerous photographs, patches, and assorted memorabilia collected during his participation in dozens of competitions. These included the Antique Aircraft Association and Experimental Aircraft Association competitions, as well as national air shows in Florida, Nevada, Texas, Maryland, and Kansas. Krier also represented the United States as a member of its aerobatic team at international championship competitions in Spain, Germany, and Russia. He was a tireless worker for the Aerobatic Club of America and was elected its president; he devoted much time and effort in this post to winning support for the U.S. team in its efforts to wrest the world championship from the European nations which had traditionally held it.

The museum contains a souvenir and book shop and there is a snack bar next door and a restaurant directly across the street.

Location: The Harold Krier Field Aerobatic Museum is on the north side of Route 160 in Ashland, Kansas. In the southwest part of the state, Ashland is about 51 miles south of Dodge City and about 157 miles west of Wichita. There is plenty of free parking space on the west side of the building. Harold Krier Field has two grass runways and visiting aircraft are welcome.

Schedule: 10 a.m. to 6 p.m. from June through September, and 12:30 p.m. to 5 p.m. from October through May. Special arrangements for tour groups. Air shows are held occasionally to benefit the museum.

Admission: Free; contributions to assist in maintaining and developing the museum are accepted.

Henry Ford Museum
Dearborn, Michigan

A visitor would need several days to see most of the extraordinary exhibits in the 14-acre Henry Ford Museum and at nearby Greenfield Village, which has more than 100 buildings scattered across its neatly landscaped 260 acres.

A very small part of the museum is devoted to aviation, but the collection which has been assembled includes so many historic aircraft in superb condition that it ranks among the foremost in the country. It also stands within walking distance of where Ford Trimotor planes were once built.

In Greenfield Village, the original Wright Brothers cycle shop and family home have been transplanted from Dayton, Ohio. The former contains many of Orville and Wilbur Wright's tools, their first wind tunnel and various furnishings, for it was in this building that the brothers developed their theories of flight, tested them, and made many of the parts that went into their first aircraft.

The museum and village were founded in 1929, although Henry Ford had been collecting artifacts of early and modern Americana for two decades. Today, the facilities are operated as a non-profit educational institution. The Robert Tannahill Memorial Library, with some 250,000 items, is associated with the museum. There are four book shops and souvenir counters to serve visitors, as well as four cafeterias and restaurants and three snack bars.

Suspended in the foreground is a 1909 Bleroit XI, companion aircraft to the one which made the first crossing of the English Channel. Behind it is a 1915 Laird biplane. (Courtesy of the Henry Ford Museum.)

Of the more than two dozen aircraft located in the transportation wing behind the arts, crafts, and trades section, a 1909 Bleriot XI monoplane of the type which first flew the English Channel is the oldest. Close by is a 1915 Laird biplane, the first aircraft ever to "loop-the-loop." E.M. Laird used the aircraft for numerous demonstration flights around the United States, and in 1917 it made an exhibition tour of China and Japan. Other planes of the same period include a 1916 Standard J–1, last flown in the Cleveland Air Races of 1934 by Ernest C. Hall; a 1916 Curtiss Seagull flying boat with gleaming mahogany and plywood fuselage; and a 1917 model Curtiss JN–4 Jenny.

The planes first used to fly over both the North and South Poles are in the museum's collection. The first is a Fokker F VIII, the *Josephine Ford,* in which Admiral Richard E. Byrd and crew flew over the North Pole on May 5, 1926. The second is the 1929 Ford Trimotor, *Floyd Bennett,* which Bennett piloted with Admiral Byrd and crew over the South Pole for the first time on November 29, 1929.

Another unique aircraft is the 1928 Junkers, *Bremen,* which made the first westbound crossing of the Atlantic Ocean on April 12–13, 1928, with a crew of two German pilots and one Irish pilot.

One aircraft of the same era, which is suspended from the roof, might have been mass-produced had it not been for a tragic accident. The little Ford *Flivver,* with a wingspan of less than 23 feet, could cruise at 100 miles an hour. The single-seat craft, powered by an all-magnesium 40 h.p. engine, was intended to become the "Model T of the Air" in Henry Ford's entry into the general aviation field. When Ford's chief test pilot and close friend, Harry Brooks, was killed testing one of the first three built, Ford discontinued its development and later gave up building aircraft altogether.

Early commercial aviation is represented by a 1927 Boeing 40 B–2, one of the 32 delivered to United Air Lines for transcontinental airmail and passenger service. It was used on the first such regularly scheduled route. 1927 was also the year that Charles A. Lindbergh made the first solo transatlantic flight in the *Spirit of St. Louis.* Although the original hangs in the Smithsonian Institution in Washington, a duplicate Ryan NYP monoplane, rebuilt in 1957, is in the Henry Ford museum. It was used in the filming of the movie, *Spirit of St. Louis,* and subsequently donated to the museum by actor James Stewart.

Two rotary wing aircraft are of particular interest. The 1931 Pitcairn Autogiro, Model PCA–2, was the first such craft built for commercial use in the United States and served as a camera plane for the *Detroit News* for a number of years. Also in the collection is Igor Sikorsky's first practical helicopter, the Vought–Sikorsky VS–300, which first flew in 1939 with the designer piloting it. It was the forerunner of a long line of military and commercial helicopters which the designer would produce.

Other noteworthy craft include the tiny 1920 Baumann RB racing plane, the first aircraft to use retractable landing gear; as well as a Zoegling glider; a Stinson Detroiter which flew around the world (excluding the Pacific) in 18 days in 1927. Also included is another Stinson Detroiter which made the world's first diesel flight the following year.

Mounted engine blocks are grouped around the planes and include a 1910 Elbridge aircraft engine, a Pratt & Whitney

The first aircraft to fly over the North Pole was this Fokker F VIII which was used on the Artic expedition of Admiral Richard E. Byrd in 1926. (Courtesy of the Henry Ford Museum.)

The emphasis is on historical interest in the aviation section of the Henry Ford Museum. Famous aircraft draw the attention of thousands of visitors every year. (Courtesy of the Henry Ford Museum.)

Wasp, a 1916 Clerget, a 1917 V–12 Liberty manufacturd by Lincoln Motor Company, Ford's experimental X–types, Lawrence, Packard diesel, Curtiss OX–5, a Gnome rotary, Hall Scott, Sturtevant of 1917, and a 1916 Hispano-Suiza. Other exhibits in the section include models and parapher-nalia such as goggles, helmets, and belts, propellors, cylinder castings, and trophies.

Location: The Henry Ford Museum and Greenfield Village can be reached on Oakwood Boulevard and the Southfield Service Drive in Dearborn, Michigan, both easily accessible from Interstate 75 and Interstate 96 on the Southfield Freeway. There is ample free parking.

Schedule: Open daily from 9 a.m. to 5 p.m. during the winter and from 9 a.m. to 6 p.m. during the summer months.

Admission: $2.75 for adults at each museum; children ages 6 to 12 at $1.25 each; children five years old and younger admitted free. Groups rates are available for senior citizens, educational, and other groups at reduced prices.

The weapons of the Strategic Air Command—bombers and missiles—are on static display outside the Aerospace Museum building. Twenty-five aircraft and seven missiles may be viewed. (Photo by John Walton, Jr.)

Strategic Aerospace Museum
Bellevue, Nebraska

Because of its capability of delivering America's slim arsenal of nuclear weapons during the years immediately after World War II, Winston Churchill once credited the Strategic Air Command with being the major single factor that deterred World War III. For more than 25 years, deterrence has been SAC's job and the organization does not take its motto "Peace Is Our Profession" lightly.

The Strategic Air Command has long flown many of the most magnificent flying machines built and has added an inventory of intercontinental range ballistic missiles to its force. It's always been one of the more glamorous, yet also serious, parts of the U.S. Air Force, with traditions reaching back into World War II. Those years were captured on film in such movies as *Twelve O'Clock High* and *Command Decision.* Actor James Stewart, himself a former bomber pilot and reserve general, appeared in the later film, *Strategic Air Command,* which stressed the professional and complex aspects of peacetime deterrence.

The first steps toward establishing a Strategic Aerospace Museum came in 1959 when General Thomas A. Power was SAC's commander-in-chief. A section of inactive runway at the command's headquarters, Offutt Air Force Base, Nebraska, was set aside and the first aircraft, a Consolidated Vultee B–36 Peacemaker, arrived in May of that year. The largest operational aircraft ever built, it was a fitting beginning, for between 1948 and 1958, when SAC operated as many as 385 of them, it never dropped a bomb or fired a shot in conflict.

The next two exhibits to be added, first in 1965, then in January, 1966, were the command's first operational Boeing B–52 Stratofortress, and a Convair Atlas ICBM which had previously stood in front of the command's headquarters building.

The museum was officially dedicated on Armed Forces Day, 1966, and discussions were started with the State of Nebraska which would eventually lead to the facility being operated as an historic park. The State assumed responsibility for operating the museum in July, 1971, and it is administered by the Division of Travel and Tourism of the Nebraska Department of Economic Development.

The outdoor exhibit area has expanded and today includes a total of 25 aircraft and seven missiles. Not only bombers, but also fighters, transports, tankers, trainers, helicopters, and rescue aircraft may be seen. The museum is situated on a 42-acre tract of land at the end of the unused runway originally set aside for the facility.

A 22,000-square-foot building has been added to house numerous historical exhibits, as well as the museum's small theatre, administrative offices, and gift shop. Among artifacts which are displayed are aircraft engines, guns, bombsights, and replicas of the nuclear weapons dropped in World War II, as well as survival equipment, navigators' sextants and electronics equipment, and selected works from the U.S. Air Force art collection. One display is devoted to the noted cigar-chewing General Curtis E. LeMay, longtime commander-in-chief of the Strategic Air Command and later Air Force chief of staff.

In addition to the aircraft which arrived prior to the opening of the museum, others which have been added are the Boeing B–17 Flying Fortress, the Douglas A–26 Invader, the North American RB–45C Tornado, the Martin B–57 Intruder, the Convair B–58 Hustler, the Boeing B–47 Stratojet, the Boeing B–29 Superfortress, and the North American B–25 Mitchell.

Cargo and transport aircraft include the Douglas C–47 Skytrain, military version of the perennial DC–3; the Douglas

Strategic Aerospace Museum's 22,000-square-foot building contains weapons, bombsights, engines, navigation equipment, and memorabilia related to U.S. Air Force bombardment units. (Courtesy of the U.S. Air Force.)

C–54 Skymaster, military version of the DC–4; the Boeing
KC–97 Stratofreighter, which was used as an aerial tanker; the
Douglas C–124 Globemaster; the Douglas C–133 Cargomas-
ter; and the Fairchild C–119 Flying Boxcar.

The four fighter aircraft on display are the Republic
RF–84F Thunderflash tactical reconnaissance aircraft; the
McDonnell F–101 Voodoo; the Convair F–102A Delta
Dagger; and the North American F–86H Sabrejet, of which
some 6000 planes were produced and which served not only
with the U.S. Air Force but also with the air forces of
numerous foreign nations. One unusual aircraft which is
included is the XF–85 Goblin, designed and built by
McDonnell Aircraft Company for use as an escort fighter for
heavy bombers. It was conceived as a "parasite" fighter which
could be carried on a bomber, then released if enemy aircraft
were encountered. Only two prototype aircraft were
produced, testing proved the concept unsatisfactory, and the
project was abandoned in 1950. The other specimen is at the
Air Force Museum in Dayton, Ohio.

Helicopters and rescue aircraft at the Strategic Aerospace
Museum are the Sikorsky UH/HH–19 Chickasaw, the Boeing
CH–21 Workhorse, and the Grumman HU–16B Albatross, a
longtime rescue amphibian credited with saving some 900
lives during the Korean War and almost as many more in
Vietnam.

The museum's missile collection includes, in addition to
the Atlas, a Bomarc surface-to-air missile, a North American
Hound Dog air-to-surface missile, a Northrop Snark intercontinental missile, a Douglas SM–75 Thor intermediate range
ballistic missile, and a Martin–Marietta Titan I intercontinental range ballistic missile.

Not a weapon, but an interesting scientific launch vehicle,
the Chance Vought SLV–1 Blue Scout has been used to put
military and NASA payloads into earth orbit.

Location: The Strategic Aerospace Museum is in Bellevue,
Nebraska, at the northern edge of Offutt Air Force Base. It can
be reached by leaving Interstate 80 in Omaha and traveling
six miles south on Routes 73 and 75. The museum is identified
with several well-situated signs. Adequate parking space is
available, and there is a small park adjacent to the museum
suitable for picnic lunches.

The Strategic Aerospace Museum is located near Offutt Air Force Base, headquarters of the Strategic Air Command. Since 1972 it has been operated by the Division of Travel and Tourism of the State of Nebraska. (Photo by John Walton, Jr.)

Schedule: Open from 8 a.m. to 5 p.m. seven days a week. Closed on Christmas Day, New Year's Day, and Easter Sunday. Special arrangements for large groups are not required.

Admission: $1.00 for adults; 50 cents for children ages six through 15; preschool children admitted free. For organized groups of 10 or more, rates are 75 cents each for adults, 35 cents each for students ages six through 15.

Aircraft suspended from the ceiling and a few of the more than two dozen aircraft engines exhibited at Pioneer Village are housed along with hundreds of vehicles. The Village has a total of 23 buildings and over 30,000 items on display. (Courtesy of the Howard Warp Pioneer Village.)

Harold Warp Pioneer Village
Minden, Nebraska

When the country schoolhouse he had attended as a boy was put up for sale in 1948, Howard Warp decided to preserve it and to develop in his hometown of Minden, Nebraska, a Pioneer Village, which was destined to become one of the state's major tourist attractions.

The 20-acre site he acquired on Route 6 now contains 23 buildings. In addition to the schoolhouse, he has added an 1884 church building, a fire house, a railway station, a two-story log fort built in 1869, a Pony Express station, barns, stables, and buildings to house more than 30,000 items. There's even a Pioneer Motel and Restaurant to serve passing tourists.

While the village contains an extensive collection of antique automobiles, motorcycles, locomotives, boats, and innumerable historical artifacts, Warp has not overlooked the history of aviation. Himself a pilot in the 1920s, he has acquired a total of 16 aircraft and 26 engines for display, as well as a number of artifacts connected with early aviation.

Harold Warp's Pioneer Village has something for everyone and it's a busy place during the summer season with a full-time staff of some 30 people. A number of them are craftsmen who work in the 14 craft shops producing souvenirs such as rugs, brooms, toys, and other items.

Most of the aircraft which can be seen are suspended from

This Hartman monoplane was built in 1910 by A. J. Hartman from a news photograph he had seen of Louis Bleriot's crossing of the English Channel. Its first flight was on May 10, 1910; its last flight, also with Hartman at the controls, was on June 19, 1955. It was powered by an Anzani engine. (Courtesy of the Howard Warp Pioneer Village.)

the roof of the building which houses more than 250 antique automobiles. However, they are definitely classic machines.

On display are a replica of the Wright Brothers 1903 Flyer, a 1910 Curtiss Hamilton, a 1910 Hartman Monoplane, a 1911 Curtiss, a 1917 JN–4 Jenny, a 1918 Lincoln Standard, a 1926 Swallow Biplane, a 1928 Cessna Model A, a 1928 Lincoln Paige Biplane, a 1929 DeHavilland Gypsy Moth, a 1930 Stinson Junior, a 1930 Pitcairn Autogiro, a 1942 Sikorsky Y–4 Helicopter, a 1942 Bell P–59 and a 1937 Taylor Cub.

The engine collection includes a 1905 Curtiss, a 1908 Wright, a 1910 Rotary Gnome, a 1914 LeRhone Rotary, a 1914 Anzani, a 1916 Hall Scott, a 1916 Lawrence, a 1917 OX–5, a 1917 Hisso, a 1918 Comet 7, a 1918 Hispano, a 1918 Liberty, a 1928 Wright, a 1929 Warner, a 1929 DeHavilland H–60, a 1929 Radial Packard Diesel, a 1930 Continental A–40, a 1938 Continental, and a 1938 Pratt & Whitney Wasp. Also included are a 1940 Lycoming, a 1940 Allison V–12, a 1940 Daimler–Benz, a 1942 J–31, a 1942 Wright, a 1942 General Electric GE–116 Turbojet, and a 1944 Wasp.

Warp himself left Minden in 1924 as a young man and successfully sought his fortune in Chicago. He founded his own company, Flex–O–Glass, Inc., which sells window covering materials throughout the world. For the past 25 years he has invested heavily in Pioneer Village, which has received more than a few awards from his home state of Nebraska where he grew up as the son of a Norwegian immigrant.

Location: The Harold Warp Pioneer Village is on Routes 6 and 34 in Minden, Nebraska, about 130 miles west of Lincoln and 14 miles south of Kearney, Nebraska. It is shown on most highway maps.

Schedule: Open seven days a week from 8 a.m. to sundown.

Admission: $1.50 for adults, 50 cents for children over six years of age. Preschool children admitted free. Special rates are available for large groups.

One of the air racing "greats" of the 1930s was Roscoe Turner's Wendell-Williams' "Special" which won the Thompson Trophy Race three times between 1932 and 1939, as well as the 1933 Bendix Race. (Photo by Elroy Sanford.)

Frederick C. Crawford
Auto-Aviation Museum
Cleveland, Ohio

The Frederick C. Crawford Auto-Aviation Museum is one of several museums in which aircraft share space with other forms of transportation—usually automobiles—and it is certainly one of the more interesting of this type.

The museum is part of the Western Reserve Historical Society, an organization formed in 1867. The auto and aviation collection, known first as the Thompson Auto Album and Aviation Museum, and later as the TRW Collection, was added to the Society's block-long museum and library facilities in the University Circle section of Cleveland in 1965.

The Thompson collection had its beginnings in 1937 when Frederick C. Crawford, president and later chairman of the executive committee of TRW Inc., acquired a 1910 automobile from an exhibitor at the 1937 Great Lakes Exposition. This subsequently sparked an interest in acquiring additional vintage automobiles and aircraft, which remained in storage until they could be exhibited for the first time in temporary quarters in 1943.

Although the more than 130 automobiles in the museum far outnumber the aircraft, the latter collection is interesting in several respects because of its local interest. Ohio figured prominently in aviation during the 1920s and 1930s and Cleveland in particular was the scene of many noteworthy events, included its famous air races. The Thompson Trophy was established in 1930 to foster the development of higher aircraft speeds combined with safety and maneuverability. One of the museum's displays is a complete collection of models of all Thompson Trophy winners, along with films, prints, photos, and books on the history of the races, as well as the trophy itself.

One outstanding feature in the museum is the complete collection of original aircraft paintings by Charles E. Hubbell, a native of Cleveland. These were commissioned by TRW Inc. as early as 1934 for a calendar series which later became known as the "Panorama of Flight." They are displayed in the area surrounding the aircraft exhibits.

Aircraft included in the museum's collection are a Curtiss Pusher of 1910, which was modified as a seaplane in 1912. Named the *Bumblebee,* it flew in Cleveland in the pre-World War I period. Two other Curtiss aircraft are the Curtiss Oriole Model 519 and a Curtiss 1917 Model F flying boat, and there is a Thomas-Morse Scout of World War I and a P–51 Mustang

The P–51K Mustang in the Crawford Auto-Aviation Museum was powered by a Packard-Rolls-Royce engine in the 1946 Thompson Trophy Race. It was rated as the fastest piston-driven built. (Photo by Elroy Sanford.)

One of the several Curtiss aircraft in the Crawford Auto-Aviation Museum is the beautifully restored 1917 Model F flying boat with mahogany main structure. (Photo by Elroy Sanford.)

fighter which was used for racing after World War II in the Thompson Trophy race of 1946. Named *Second Fiddle,* it was piloted by Bob Swanson.

Another Thompson Trophy aircraft is Roscoe Turner's Wedell–Williams Special which participated in the races from 1932 to 1939, winning the Thompson Trophy three times. It held the transcontinental speed record in 1933.

Location: The Frederick C. Crawford Auto-Aviation Museum is located at 10825 East Boulevard in Cleveland.

Schedule: Open Tuesday through Saturday from 10 a.m. to 5 p.m. , and on Sunday from 1 p.m. to 6 p.m. Closed Mondays.

Admission: 50 cents for adults; 25 cents for children over 6 and for students. Organized groups by appointment and members free. Tuesdays free to all.

This sixty by twenty foot mosaic mural in the Dayton Convention and Exhibition Center depicts the Wright Brothers' first flight. The Aviation Hall of Fame is located on the balcony above the mural. (Photo by Jon Allen.)

Aviation Hall of Fame
Dayton, Ohio

A few miles from the location of Wilbur and Orville Wright's original bicycle shop in Dayton, Ohio, stands the city's modern Convention and Exhibition Center. Occupying an entire city block, it was opened to the public in January, 1973.

The building's third floor, reached by escalator from the lobby, houses the Aviation Hall of Fame.

The lobby itself is dominated by a mosaic mural, 60 feet wide by 20 feet high, depicting the Wright Brothers' first flight on December 17, 1903. Facing each other across the lobby are busts of the two brothers, spaced exactly 120 feet apart, the distance covered by Orville Wright during the 12 second span of man's first powered flight. The mural is actually composed of 163,000 one-inch-square mosaic tiles. Titled *First Flight* it was designed by Read Viemeister and presented to the city by the Rike Family Foundation of Dayton.

The Aviation Hall of Fame was formally organized in 1962 through the efforts of the aviation committee of the Dayton Area Chamber of Commerce and was chartered by an Act of Congress two years later. A 36-member board of trustees administers the Hall of Fame.

Since 1962, a total of 53 aviation pioneers have been enshrined in the Aviation Hall of Fame. Their portraits, sketched by aviation artist Milton Caniff, hang on the third floor of the Convention and Exhibition Center, along with citations describing their achievements.

The organization holds an awards banquet each year in Dayton at which the new enshrinees are announced. The events are generally attended by numerous notables in the field of aviation, and honorary chairmen of the dinners in recent years have been personalities with strong aviation connections, including Arthur Godfrey, actor James Stewart, Hugh Downs, and Senator Barry Goldwater.

The Aviation Hall of Fame publishes a quarterly membership newsletter which is sent to individual and organization members. It also has gold, silver, and bronze medals of the Hall of Fame enshrinees available for sale. Memberships and medals both help support the Hall of Fame, which is a non-profit organization.

Portraits and citations of the 53 men and women who have been honored by the Aviation Hall of Fame may be seen in the Dayton Convention and Exhibition Center. The portraits are by artist Milton Caniff. (Photo by Jon Allen.)

Entrance to the Dayton Convention and Exhibition Center which leads to the Aviation Hall of Fame. The first flight mural and busts of Wilbur and Orville Wright dominate the lobby. (Photo by Jon Allen.)

While the central purpose of the Aviation Hall of Fame is to pay tribute to these who have been enshrined, future plans call for collecting memorabilia and expanding display areas to become more of a museum.

A number of other aviation organizations have already expressed interest in co-locating in Dayton with the Aviation Hall of Fame, so a shared museum facility may become an eventual reality in the city which terms itself the "birthplace of aviation."

Location: The Aviation Hall of Fame is located in the Dayton Convention and Exhibition Center at the corner of Main and Fifth Streets. The city's transportation center across the street provides ample parking space. Motorists arriving in Dayton on Interstate 75 can exit right on Main Street.

Schedule: The Aviation Hall of Fame area of the building's third floor is open from 9 a.m. to 6 p.m. every day.

Admission: Free.

With 80 aircraft displayed inside and some 30 additional larger models outside on the "flight line," the Air Force Museum is the largest, most complete facility of its kind in the world. (Courtesy of the U.S. Air Force.)

U.S. Air Force Museum
Wright-Patterson Air Force Base
Dayton, Ohio

With much of the nation's aviation and space progress so closely associated with the achievements of military men, it is only natural that the U.S. Air Force Museum should be one of the largest in the country. And, with close to one million visitors a year, it is certainly one of the most popular. No other military aviation museum in the world contains such comprehensive and, in many cases, unique hardware and memorabilia.

The museum's origins date back to 1923 at McCook Field, near Dayton, where combat aircraft and equipment of the United States and other nations were shown informally. From 1927 to 1935, the museum occupied 1500 square feet of space in a laboratory building at Wright Field.

A Works Project Administration (WPA) project gave the museum its first permanent home in 1935 in a specially designed building constructed at a cost of $235,000. However, during World War II, it was converted to other uses and the museum's collection of more than 2000 items was placed in storage.

The museum reopened its doors in 1954, this time situated in a temporary World War II structure. During the first year, it had 10,000 visitors. Its floor plan was designed to guide visitors through the story of military aviation, rather than simply display a collection of aircraft. This philosophy has

163

This Wright 1909 Military Flyer, purchased by the U.S. Army Signal Corps for $30,000, was the world's first military aircraft. The original is in the Smithsonian Institution; this replica was constructed in 1955 and equipped with an engine donated by Orville Wright. (Courtesy of the U.S. Air Force.)

been maintained to the present day, with the museum truly achieving educational and informative objectives, not merely serving as a repository.

The organization of the Air Force Museum Foundation as a non-profit goup in 1960 was the first step in providing a new permanent home for the museum. Its impressive building, completed at a cost of $6 million and paid for entirely by public contributions, was dedicated in September, 1971, on the Wright Field portion of Wright-Patterson Air Force Base. The museum property covers a total of 400 acres.

The Air Force Museum is under the control of the Secretary of the Air Force Office of Information, with the objective of portraying the history of the U.S. Air Force and preserving its heritage and traditions. That it does so with remarkable public appeal is indicated by the fact that it is the largest single tourist attraction in Ohio.

The museum's exhibits, of course, include military aircraft spanning the years from the time of the Wright 1909 Military Flier to the most modern supersonic jets, but its many special exhibits also illuminate Air Force history and tradition in numerous other ways. A prisoner-of-war display contains original items from Stalag Luft I at Barth, Germany, where American fliers were held during World War II. A Southeast Asia prisoner-of-war exhibit contains correspondence, crutches, sketches, and a uniform issued to an American pilot in North Vietnam. Another exhibit describes the role of the black American in military aviation, with mementos contributed by some of the more than 1000 black pilots trained at Tuskegee Field during World War II. The stories of retired and active general officers are included in the exhibit.

One exhibit area is an art gallery where selected canvases from the U.S. Air Force art collection are shown. The collection, which the Air Force has sponsored for a number of years, also has traveling units which may be seen on exhibition regularly in other museums and during special events in various parts of the country.

The Air Force Museum's building is designed somewhat like an early aviation hangar, with two spacious display areas connected by a "core " section through which visitors enter. This section contains galleries, offices, a 500-seat theatre, and a restaurant and a gift shop.

A total of 210,000 square feet of display space is available for the 80 planes which are housed inside. An additional 30-plus aircraft are on static display outside the building on the museum's "flight line."

One display area starts with the Wright Brothers period and shows activities and aircraft of the First World War, then the Army Air Corps during the 1920s and 1930s. The second, and larger, display area, starts with Pearl Harbor, illustrates the rapid development of military aviation during World War II and Korea, and includes a Space Age section.

The World War I section includes aircraft such as the Standard J-1, the Curtiss JN-4-D Jenny, the Spad VII, Thomas-Morse S4B Scout, and Standard E-1. An unusually interesting specimen is the Kettering "bug" or aerial torpedo, the world's first guided missile, which was developed for the U.S. Army Signal Corps in 1918 by the Dayton-Wright Company. It had a range of 40 miles and a warhead of 180 pounds of explosives, but World War I came to an end before it could be tested in combat.

Aircraft used between the wars which are on display include the Douglas World Cruiser, *New Orleans*, which was built in 1923 and designed to fly around the world, which it did with its sister ship, *Boston II*, in 1924, a trip of some 26,345 miles. Also included are the Consolidated PT-1, Curtiss P-6E Hawk, Boeing P-26A, Stearman PT-13D and Curtiss P-36A Hawk.

The World War II aircraft shown include fighters and bombers, trainers, observation planes and helicopters, and even a German V-1 Buzz-Bomb and a Japanese Fuji Hikoki MXY7 Okha suicide plane. Among the fighters are the Curtiss P-40N Warhawk, a British Supermarine Spitfire Mark L.F. XVIe, the Lockheed P-38L Lightning, Bell P-39Q Airacobra, Republic P-47D Thunderbolt, German Focke-Wulf FW-190D-9, North American P-51D Mustang, a Japanese Kawanishi N1K2-J Shiden-Kai "George" 21, and the North American F-82B Twin Mustang.

Leading World War II bombers on exhibit are the Boeing B-17G Flying Fortress, North American B-25B Mitchell, Douglas A-20G Havoc, Consolidated B-24D Liberator, Martin B-26G Marauder, Douglas A-26C Invader, and Boeing B-29 Superfortress.

More than 80 airplanes, including such World War II favorites as the B–17, P–38, and B–24, are displayed in the U.S. Air Force Museum's exhibit area. (Courtesy of the U.S. Air Force.)

The Japanese Fuji Hikoki MXY7 "Ohka" suicide bomb was used against U.S. warships during the last days of World War II. Powered during the last few minutes of flight by a rocket engine, it carried a warhead with over a ton of high explosives in a burst of speed—up to 600 m.p.h. (Courtesy of the U.S. Air Force.)

Jet age aircraft range from the first U.S. production model fighter, the Lockheed P–80R Shooting Star, up to experimental aircraft which were unique. Combat aircraft include the Republic F–84E Thunderjet, North American F–86A Sabre, Northrop F–89J Scorpion, Lockheed F–94 Starfire, North American F–100A Super Sabre, Convair F–106A Delta Dart, and North American F–107A. Also shown is the Russian-built Mikoyan–Gurevich MiG–15 *Fagot;* the one displayed was flown from North Korea in 1953 by a defecting pilot.

Postwar bombers which may be seen are the Convair B–36J, the Boeing B–47E Stratojet, Martin RB–57A Canberra, and Boeing B–52 Stratofortress, as well as the exotic and graceful North American XB–70 Valkyrie, of which only two were ever built. Experimental aircraft include the Bell XB–1 rocket plane, the Douglas X–3 Stiletto, the Bell X–5, North American X–10, the Ryan X–13 Vertijet, and others.

Location: The U.S. Air Force Museum is on Wright-Patterson Air Force Base, six miles northeast of Dayton. It can be reached on Interstate Highway 70 to Route 4 South, exiting at Harshman Road. On Interstate Highway 75, exit at Needmore Road east. Plenty of parking is available.

Schedule: Monday through Friday from 9 a.m. to 5 p.m. and weekends from 10 a.m. to 6 p.m. Closed Christmas Day.

Admission: Free.

Lockheed P–80 Shooting Star bears Navy markings. Although originally based at the Naval Missile Center in California, the aircraft was acquired by Soplata in Harrisburg, Pa. (Courtesy of Walter A. Soplata.)

Walter A. Soplata Collection
Newbury, Ohio

Walter A. Soplata has had a love affair with aircraft since he saw his first one as a small boy in Cleveland. He learned to fly in Chagrin Falls, Ohio, in 1944 and received his aircraft and engine mechanic's license two years later.

He believes in saving airplanes, and he believes that seeing them up close, sitting in the cockpits, taking pictures of them, and taking measurements gives people a better understanding of aviation.

Since he acquired his first aircraft, a BT–13 without engines or instruments, for $145 in 1947, he has traveled thousands of miles, spent thousands of dollars, and added almost 40 additional aircraft to his private collection. His latest acquisition is an RB–36 for which he paid seven cents a pound and which he is moving to Newbury in parts, with an estimated 50 trips being required to transport the 98,000-pound aircraft, stripped of engines and landing gear.

Many of his aircraft are incomplete, many have survived accidents, and many have been ravaged by being stripped for salvage or to demilitarize them. As time and money permit, he and his family piece them back together again, paint them and put them into display condition. Nothing ever rots in his collection, since everything is sprayed with oil twice a year to prevent rust and corrosion until restoration work can be started.

Mr. Soplata has devoted three acres of his 18.5 acres of property to aircraft exhibits and there is a small building which is used for working on the collection. He has also accumulated a private collection of about 50,000 books and magazines which will be established as a library and catalogued for the benefit of aviation historians and other researchers.

While the Soplata Collection is not housed in a museum building or at an airport, it is known throughout the world. It is open to anyone at any time, although several days notice is appreciated if visitors would like to be shown around by a member of Mr. Soplata's family.

Aircraft which may be viewed are an F7U–3 Cutlass, a Cessna T–50, a Fairchild C–82A–44, an AD5N, a Goodyear Corsair FG1D, a Goodyear Corsair F2G which won the 1947 Thompson Trophy Race, a Lockheed P–80–1–60, a Lockheed T–33A, a North American B–25J, a North American T–28A, a North American P–82E, a Vultee Valiant BT–15 and a BT–13A, an RF–84F, and a Fleetwing YBT–12.

North American P–82 Twin Mustang is one of the few of its type preserved in a museum or private collection. (Courtesy of Walter A. Soplata.)

Also included in the collection are a Curtiss O–52 Owl, a Grumman TBM–3, a Douglas B–26, a Republic P–47N, a KC–97, an XBT2D, a Neptune P2V–7, an RB–36, a Bell P–63, a North American P–51K, a Grumman F–11F, a Sikorsky HSS–1, and two F–86 Sabrejets, a North American AT–6G, the BT–13, and an F2H.

Location: Newbury, Ohio is about 25 miles east of Cleveland on Routes 44 and 87. From Route 87, Stone Road leads to Restful Lake. A left turn on the first road past the lake takes the visitor along a 500-foot private road to the Walter A. Soplata Collection. Parking is available for up to a dozen cars in dry weather.

Schedule: Open daily all year. A few days notice is suggested if visitors would like to be shown around by Mr. Soplata or a member of his family.

Admission: Free.

The unique "mound" design of the Neil Armstrong Air and Space Museum permits freedom in the use of interior space without regard for outside appearance. Exhibit areas cover a total of 14,000 square feet. (Courtesy of the Ohio Historical Society.)

Armstrong Air and Space Museum Wapakoneta, Ohio

A string of airport runway lights guides visitors into the entrance to the Neil Armstrong Air and Space Museum in Wapakoneta, Ohio. The unique "mound" structure, with 14,000 square feet of interior display space, was opened to the public on July 20, 1972, the third anniversary of Armstrong's first step on the surface of the moon.

The museum is in the form of a series of planned multi-level exhibits around a central "astro-theatre" which is topped by a 60-foot diameter dome. In here, a total of nine slide and motion picture projectors operate continuously to present a sight and sound panorama of the contributions made by the State of Ohio to manned flight.

Museum planners designed the facility to give visitors a "total experience" and refer to the lounge and garden area at the conclusion of a visit as a form of "decompression area" where one may get back to earth and browse among the mementos and art which recall Neil Armstrong's exploration of the moon.

Since the museum is named for Armstrong and he spent much of his early life in the community, a number of exhibits naturally relate to the astronaut, starting with boyhood items which indicate his early interest in aviation. These include models which he built and the 1946 Aeronca 7AC Champion training aircraft in which he learned to fly as a teenager. In contrast with this is an F5D Skylancer jet, exhibited on a pad at the entrance to the museum, which Armstrong flew while assigned to the National Aeronautics and Space Administration during the early 1960s.

An elevated gallery above the first hall in the museum contains the actual Gemini VIII spacecraft in which Armstrong and David Scott orbited the earth in the first space docking mission in March, 1966. A good view of the interior is made possible by removal of the command pilot's access hatch, and a videotape of the Gemini VIII mission plays directly above for visitors. Armstrong's original Gemini VIII space suit is also shown.

As one enters the museum, panels of photographs trace the development of manned flight from Kitty Hawk to the Sea of Tranquility. One section, covering the history of flight in Ohio and contributions made by natives of the state, includes the *Toledo II* airship built by A. Roy Knabenshue in 1905, as well as a Model G Wright Brothers flying boat built in Dayton and flown by Ernest Hall in 1913. The early ballooning era is recalled with a basket, equipment, and memorabilia belonging to Warren Rasor of Dayton.

Because so much documentation of space flight, from the Mercury program through Skylab, is on videotape, a special room with three television monitors shows continuous programs of missions carried out by Armstrong and other astronauts. To give the visitor an idea of the infinite distances in space, an entirely mirrored room takes him into the

Gemini VIII spacecraft in which Astronauts Neil Armstrong and David Scott orbited the earth in the world's first space docking mission in March, 1966. Video tape above the capsule tells the story of the Gemini VIII mission. (Courtesy of the Ohio Historical Society.)

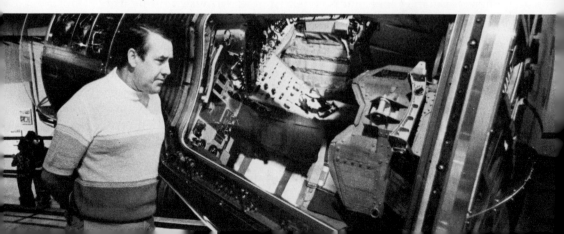

The early days of flight in Ohio are featured in the first gallery of the Armstrong Museum. Included are the *Toledo II* airship, built in 1905, and the Wright Brothers' Model G Aero-boat, built in Dayton in 1913. A slide show entitled *Up, Up, and Away* tells the story of lighter-than-air flight in Ohio. (Courtesy of the Ohio Historical Society.)

"'astro-theatre." Passing through this 18-foot square cube, he can see his own reflection projected to infinity.

The Armstrong Museum is operated by the Ohio Historical Society. The decision to construct it was announced by the governor only a few hours after Armstrong walked for the first time on the moon. Although the Ohio General Assembly appropriated $500,000 toward its construction, a private fund-raising campaign was even more successful. Some 2500 contributors, mostly in Ohio and particularly in counties surrounding Wapakoneta, pledged a total of $544,000. The museum stands on a 13-acre site next to Interstate Highway 75. Another native of Wapakoneta, Arthur Klipfel, Jr., now of Cambridge, Massachusetts and a graduate of the Yale architecture school, served as design consultant for the building itself and the interior exhibit areas.

Location: The Armstrong Air and Space Museum is situated on Interstate Highway 75 at Exit 65 (Fisher–Wapak Road). Wapakoneta is in western Ohio, approximately 58 miles north of Dayton and 94 miles south of Toledo.

Schedule: Open Monday through Saturday from 9:30 a.m. to 5 p.m. and on Sundays and holidays from 1 p.m. to 5 p.m. Closed Thanksgiving Day, Christmas Day, and New Year's Day.

Admission: $1.00 for adults; 50 cents for children. School groups admitted free.

The EAA has its own headquarters building adjacent to the museum. The organization has three divisions: International Aerobatic Club, Inc., Warbirds of America, Inc., and the Antique and Classic Division. (Photo by Lee Fray.)

EAA Aviation Museum
Franklin, Wisconsin

The Experimental Aircraft Association's two locations in Franklin and Burlington, Wisconsin, comprise the most extensive facility of this type in operation today. The organization has a total of seven buildings, situated on 64 acres of land.

The EAA Museum is in Franklin, on a 14-acre site, and contains 40,000 square feet of display space, with over 120 aircraft exhibited. Some 40 additional aircraft are under construction or restoration, or are in temporary storage. An excellent museum sales store is maintained and a research library is available to the museum staff. The organization's Flight Test Center is on a 50-acre property at Burlington Municipal Airport.

The museum's aircraft collection includes just about every type of plane, other than larger commercial or military aircraft. There are custom-built aircraft, antiques and classics, aerobatic and show aircraft, military planes, gliders, rotary wings, racers, balloons, and drones. In addition to original models, a number of carefully constructed, completely authentic reproductions of famous planes may be seen. More than 40 aircraft engines of various types are exhibited, and an additional 30 are in storage awaiting display.

Many of the museum's more than 30,000 visitors a year are children from the school districts in and around Milwaukee.

179

Many EAA Museum aircraft are one-of-a-kind specimens, restored and maintained in superb condition. They include antiques, classics, aerobatic and racing planes, gliders, and aircraft of both World Wars. (Photo by Dick Stouffer.)

More than 120 aircraft are displayed in the EAA Museum. Members of the staff and volunteers constantly participate in restoration projects. (Photo by Dick Stouffer.)

Educational activities are viewed as an important part of the Museum Foundation's objectives, and a program titled "Project Schoolflight" is conducted to provide aviation-oriented materials and projects to various schools.

Ten aircraft in the EAA Museum collection are currently flying: a P–8 Acro Sport, a Grumman J2F–6 Duck, a Lincoln PTK, a North American AT–6D and SNJ–5, a North American P–51D Mustang and P–64, a Pitts P–7 Special, a Vultee BT–13B, and a Waco UPF–7.

Antique and classic aircraft exhibited are an Aeronca C–3 Collegian and a C–3 Master, a Curtiss E–8.75 Sweetheart, a Curtiss C–1 Robin, a DeHavilland 82C Tiger Moth, a Fairchild FC–2, a Fairchild 22C7A, a Goodyear GA–22 Drake, a Monocoupe 90A and 113, a Nicholas–Beazley NB–8G, a Pheasant H–10, a Pietenpol B4A–1 Scout, a Rearwin 7000 Sportster, a Royal Aircraft Factory S.E.5a, a Ryan NYP, and a Taylor E–2 Cub.

Aerobatic and show aircraft include a Bucker 133 Jungmeister, a Champion 8KCAB Pro, a DeHavilland DHC–1B–2 Chipmunk, and a Grumman G–22A Gulfhawk 2.

Racing aircraft include a Church JC–1 Midwing, an Elmendorf Special Jackrabbit, a Loving WR–1 Love, a North American P–51D Mustang, a Petit Special, and a Wittman Bonzo.

Military aircraft which can be seen indoors include a Bell P–39Q Airacobra, a Curtiss O–52 Owl, two Globe drones, a Nakagima K1.43–2 Oscar, a North American P–51D Mustang, and two Radioplane drones, an OQ–2A and an OQ–19D.

Outdoor display aircraft are a Baumann B–290 Brigadier, a Douglas AD–3, a Douglas AD–5, a Lockheed GF–80C, a pair of Lockheed T–33A trainers, a North American F–86H, a Northrup F–89J, and a Republic F–84C and F–84F.

Aircraft which are unique or distinctive in the museum include a 1911 Curtiss E–8.75 Pusher, the oldest flyable aircraft in the U.S.; a 1952 Stits SA–2A Skybaby, the world's smallest man-carrying aircraft; and a Junkers JU–87R–2 Stuka divebomber, oldest of only three such remaining in the world.

Rounding out the diverse collection are the numerous custom-built aircraft, as well as seven gliders, a few helicopters and a variety of unclassified planes, including an exquisite one-quarter scale Fokker D–VII, and some balloons.

The Museum Foundation launched a fund-raising program

The EAA Museum stresses its educational role. Thousands of school children from the greater Milwaukee area are among its 30,000 yearly visitors. (Photo by Lee Fray.)

among Experimental Aircraft Association members and others interested in aviation history early in 1974 to expand the museum facilities. A goal of $169,000 was established to expand display space, add additional shop area, and a library and auditorium.

The Experimental Aircraft Association was founded in 1953 by Paul H. Poberenzy, a retired Air Force colonel who flew in World War II and the Korean War. The EAA Museum Foundation which administers the museum was established in 1964 as a non-profit educational institution. Mr. Poberenzy serves as president of the Association and as executive director of the museum foundation.

The Association has more than 30,000 members and some 480 chapters located in every state and in seven Canadian provinces. There are also eleven chapters overseas, with one each in Australia, Belgium, Italy, England, and South Africa. There are three chapters in Japan, and the Marshall Islands and the Canal Zone have one each.

The EAA has three divisions: The International Aerobatic Club, Inc., Warbirds of America, Inc., and an Antique and Classic Division. The Association publishes its own monthly magazine, *Sport Aviation,* which is included with membership. This is open to anyone with an interest in aviation, with annual dues of $15 for adults and $8 for junior members.

The Association also publishes a number of books and manuals, stocks back issues of *Sport Aviation,* and sells plans and drawings of a variety of aircraft for builders.

Location: The EAA Museum is located at 11311 West Forest Home Avenue in Franklin, Wisconsin, a suburb of Milwaukee. From Milwaukee, exit from Route 94 at Route 24; this becomes Forest Home Avenue. Franklin is a 10-minute drive from Milwaukee and about one hour north of Chicago on Route 94. The Hales Corners airstrip, less than a mile from the museum, has a 2200-foot grass runway. Mitchell Field, about 10 miles east, adjacent to Route 94, is served by major airlines. Free parking is available.

Schedule: Monday through Friday from 8:30 a.m. to 5 p.m. Saturdays from 10 a.m. to 5 p.m. Sundays and holidays from 1 p.m. to 5 p.m.. Closed Christmas Day, New Year's Day, and Easter Sunday.

Admission: $1.00 for adults, 50 cents for children and students.

SOUTHWEST

The Museum's collection numbers more than 70 aircraft. It will become the central attraction in a large recreation area to be managed by the Pima County Parks and Recreation Department. (Photo by Fred Wehrman.)

Tucson Air Museum
Tucson, Arizona

For a number of years prior to 1966, the Military Aircraft Storage and Disposition Center at Davis-Monthan Air Force Base, Arizona, maintained an informal display of aircraft near the main gate to the base. Often as many as 35 aircraft, retired from active service, could be seen.

While never intended as a museum and never opened to the public, the display invariably attracted public attention. Its popularity often caused traffic problems along Golf Links Road which skirts the base perimeter.

It seemed like a natural idea to members of the Tucson Chapter of the Air Force Association to tap the Center's excellent resources in establishing a local aviation museum available to the general public.

In 1966, when Davis-Monthan Air Force Base was observing its 25th anniversary, the idea received widespread support from local officials, aviation enthusiasts, a number of retired military officers, and the U.S. government. A Tucson Air Museum Foundation was formed within a year.

A 320-acre site owned by the Federal government was selected, with Congressman Morris K. Udall instrumental in arranging for its purchase and transfer from the Federal Bureau of Land Management to the Pima County Board of Supervisors. The County has appropriated funds on two occasions to develop the property.

A $15,000 appropriation in 1969 was used for engineering, surveying, and mapping, with an additional $50,000 the following year used for road construction, well drilling, pump and tank installation, lighting, and security fencing.

Since the original concept for the Tucson Air Museum was developed, some 30 acres have been placed in use, with an additional 50 acres in reserve. Plans for the future call for the museum area to be surrounded by a park which will feature a swimming pool, playgrounds, a model aircraft flying field, ponds, and trailer facilities.

The museum area itself will have permanent buildings, including hangars of the periods represented by various aircraft, as well as a snack shop, souvenir and book shop, and restrooms.

By the beginning of 1969, the Museum Foundation had acquired its first three aircraft: a BT–13A Vultee Vibrator, presented by the local school district; an L–5B Stinson Sentinel from the Arizona Wing of the Civil Air Patrol; and a damaged F–94A, located by a parish priest in Patagonia, Arizona. Later that year, a volunteer crew of Air Force personnel journeyed to India to fly an aging B–24J from Poona to Tucson. With en-route support from Shell Oil Company, Pan Am, TWA, General Dynamics, Pratt & Whitney, and Honeywell, the crew brought the vintage Liberator back in 31 days with a dozen stops along the way. Dubbed the *Pima Paisano*, the B–24 symbolized a giant step forward for the museum.

Before the end of 1969, the Military Aircraft Storage and Disposition Center had transferred 35 aircraft to the foundation and since then the collection has grown to almost 80 aircraft, five of them on loan from the National Air and Space Museum.

During 1973, fencing and lighting of the 30 acres already in use was completed, a well was in operation, and a trailer was placed on the property for the resident caretaker.

The museum's collection includes aircraft used by the U.S. Army Air Corps, the U.S. Air Force, the U.S. Army, the U.S. Navy, U.S. Marine Corps, Canadian Forces, and a couple of civil aircraft. Rounding out the display are a few missiles and several vehicles. Several of the aircraft currently displayed are considered unique and cannot be seen elsewhere in any museum.

The Tuscon Air Museum's 30-acre site includes military aircraft such as a WB–66D, F–102A, EB–57D, C–133A, C–97G, and F–84F. (Courtesy of the Tuscon Air Museum.)

Vintage military aircraft which are included are a B–18A, B–23, A–26C, B–24J, B–25J, B–29, UC–36A, C–46D, C–47, C–54D, C–69, C–82A, F–5G, L–2M, L–3B, L–5B, P–63E, P–84B, PQ–14B, AT–6B, AT–11, BT–13A, PT–19A, and PT–22.

The C–47 was the second aircraft of its type manufactured and it served with the French Air Force; the C–69 is the sole surviving one of this type; and the C–82A is the only museum specimen of this aircraft. The P–84B is the oldest surviving P–84.

Air Force aircraft of more recent vintage include an A–26A, B–47E, WB–50D, KB–50J, EB–57D, B–58A, RB–66B, WB–66D, C–97G, KC–97G, C–119C, C–121A, EC–121H, C–124C, YC–125A, C–133A, C–133B, RF–84F, F–84F, F–86L, F–86H, F–89J, F–94A, F–94C, F–102A, H–5G, and SA–16A.

The B–57 is the only one currently in a museum, while the B–58 is the last production model manufactured.

Navy and Marine Corps aircraft are an FB–5, AD–5N, A3D–1, A4D–2, F3D–2, F4D–1, F9F–8, F9F–8P, F11F–1 (two), F3H–2, FJ–4B, F8U–1, HOK–1, HTL–7, P2V–7, PBM–5A, R4D–8, R50–5, SNB–5, SNJ–5B, and a T2V–1. Army aircraft are an H–19D, H–21C, H–34A, and H–37B.

Both civil aircraft are unique museum specimens; the Boeing S–307, formerly of Pan American Airways and the Haitian Air Force, is the only specimen in a museum, as is the Waco ZKS–6.

The Tucson Air Museum has received considerable support from the community, as well as the cooperation of the National Air and Space Museum and the armed forces aviation museums. It has become the largest collection in the Western U.S. in a relatively short time, and with the unique resources of the Military Aircraft Storage and Disposition Center to draw upon, seems assured of select specimens for future growth.

Location: Immediately south of Davis–Monthan Air Force Base, near the intersection of South Wilmot Road and Old Vail Road. Easily accessible from Interstate 10, via the Wilmot exit.

Schedule: 10 a.m. to 8 p.m. Saturdays and Sundays.

Admission: $1.00.

National Atomic Museum
Albuquerque, New Mexico

Twenty years ago, student officers in the U.S. Air Force with an appropriate security clearance received a short course of instruction on the development and handling of nuclear weapons. Occasionally, it seemed that the curriculum might have been taken, for the most part, out of the news magazines of the day, although the details, in retrospect, did justify coverage of the entire course with a "secret" classification.

Today, any tourist traveling Route 66 across northern New Mexico can find out almost as much about nuclear weapons development by detouring less than two miles on Wyoming Boulevard for a visit to the National Atomic Museum on the outskirts of Albuquerque.

Here may be seen mockups of "Little Boy" and "Fat Man"—the first and only atomic bombs ever used in warfare. The first was dropped, without ever being tested, on Hiroshima, Japan, on August 6, 1945, from the B–29 *Enola Gay* and detonated at an altitude of 1870 feet. "Fat Man" was dropped three days later on Nagasaki.

Both, unquestionably, were primarily responsible for the swift conclusion of World War II on September 2 and for saving thousands of lives; their use was a momentous decision which faced President Truman less than four months after he assumed office.

Established in October, 1969, as the Sandia Atomic

Replicas of the only two nuclear weapons used in warfare: "Little Boy," left, which was dropped on Hiroshima, and "Fat Man," right, which was dropped on Nagasaki. (Courtesy of the National Atomic Museum.)

Museum, the National Atomic Museum is operated by the Defense Nuclear Agency. A foundation to provide financial support for the museum was formed in August, 1973.

About 15,000 square feet of display space is available in one large and two small areas, and an 85-seat theatre is used to screen films. A small library is available for on-premises use.

The building itself was originally designed as a maintenance facility for 90mm anti-aircraft guns.

The purpose of the museum is to dispel some of the mystery surrounding nuclear weapons development and provide a better public understanding of testing programs, from the original Trinity test in New Mexico on July 16, 1945, through the South Pacific tests and later underground testing programs. One section of the exhibits is devoted to the history of testing of nuclear devices, both as military weapons and for their potential peaceful applications. Displays of models show various rockets and missiles capable of carrying nuclear warheads, as well as an explanation of the uses of nuclear energy.

In addition to "Little Boy" and "Fat Man," several other operational weapons systems are shown. These include the MK–17 bomb, one of the first thermonuclear weapons tested, which weighs 21 tons. Only the B–36 and B–52 aircraft were capable of carrying it. Also on display is the Navy's MK–101 or "Lulu," an air-launched atomic depth charge. Only 18 inches in diameter, but 7.7 feet in length, it weighs 1200 pounds.

The largest exhibit on display is the Army's 280mm cannon, capable of firing a 600-pound nuclear or conventional projectile for a distance of 20 miles. With the vehicles required to carry it, the cannon weighs some 86 tons, of which the barrel alone accounts for 21 tons. It is 41 feet long.

Another Army weapon is the "Little John," a free-flight rocket, powered by a solid fuel single-stage engine, with a range of more than 10 miles. The 800-pound missile was launched from a portable launcher and was highly mobile and capable of being transported into the field by helicopter. It was deployed with U.S. forces in the United States and overseas during the late 1950s.

The National Atomic Museum is considered to be a permanent and, at the same time, expanding exhibit of

The history of nuclear weapons testing is told in news articles and photographs at the National Atomic Museum. Opened in 1969, it is just south of Albuquerque, New Mexico. (Courtesy of the National Atomic Museum.)

unarmed bombs, missiles, rockets, and artillery pieces used by the Air Force, Navy, Army, and Marine Corps in maintaining the nation's defense posture. It serves as an educational center, with numerous schools, civic groups, and service clubs among the organized visitor groups. For special arrangements or large groups, advance notification at least two weeks ahead of time is recommended. Telephone: (505) 264–4223.

Since none of the exhibits is subject to security classification, photographs may be taken of all of the museum's contents.

North of the City of Albuquerque is the Los Alamos Scientific Laboratory, birthplace of the world's first atomic bomb, which has its own Los Alamos Scientific Museum. Sandia Laboratories also operates an exhibit center which is open to the public.

About 120 miles to the south of Albuquerque is Trinity Site, location of the world's first atomic detonation. It is within the White Sands Missile Range, a Department of Defense installation.

Location: The National Atomic Museum is on Wyoming Road, three miles south of Route 40, and less than two miles from Route 66. It is adjacent to Kirtland Air Force Base, south of Albuquerque, New Mexico. There is ample parking space in front of the museum.

Schedule: Open seven days a week, Monday through Friday from 9 a.m. to 5 p.m. and on weekends and holidays from noon to 5 p.m. Closed on Thanksgiving Day, Christmas Day, and New Year's Day.

Admission: Free.

The Goddard workshop in the Roswell Museum contains most of
the original equipment and furnishings used by the rocket pioneer
during his experiments in New Mexico between 1930 and 1942.
(Photo by Drucilla Denney.)

The Roswell Museum
Roswell, New Mexico

A major chapter in the history of rocket research was written in the Eden Valley of southeastern New Mexico, an isolated area where a dedicated scientist from Worcester, Massachusetts, proved his theoretical work.

From 1930 to 1942, Dr. Robert H. Goddard, acknowledged as the "father of modern rocketry," maintained a workshop on Mescalero Road in Roswell and launched dozens of high-altitude rockets a dozen miles away in the Eden Valley.

Today, Dr. Goddard's workshop has been completely restored and is a part of the Robert H. Goddard Rocket and Space Wing of the Roswell Museum. From 1965 to 1969, through the efforts of Dr. Goddard's widow and those of Nils Ljungquist and George Bode, two of his assistants, original machinery was obtained from the Curtiss-Wright Corporation, duplicate equipment was purchased and as many original furnishings as could be located were acquired. The workshop replica, which was dedicated in June, 1969, was financed and constructed by members of the Roswell Rotary Club, of which Dr. Goddard had been a member during his experiments in New Mexico.

Dr. Goddard first arrived in Roswell in July, 1930, and by December had launched his first liquid fuel rocket there on a flight of about one-half mile. His first success with liquid fuel rockets had come four years earlier, in 1926, but within a short

Early rocketery experiments conducted by Dr. Goddard are illustrated, along with actual components and instruments which he used. His last and most advanced launching tower may be seen outside the Roswell Museum. (U.S. Army Photogaph.)

time he realized that he required the space and isolation which he found in New Mexico for further experiments.

His pioneering work in New Mexico followed years of theoretical work which started prior to World War I when he was at Princeton University and at Clark University in Worcester, Massachusetts.

During World War I, he worked on military applications of rockets and, in fact, developed and successfully demonstrated the firing of a projectile which became the highly successful anti-tank "bazooka" of World War II the day before the Armistice was signed. During World War II, Dr. Goddard was deeply involved in liquid fuel rocket research programs for the U.S. Navy. He died in August, 1945, full of plans to return to New Mexico after the war and continue his high-altitude rocket research program.

The Goddard Rocket and Space Wing of the Roswell Museum, which covers about 1800 square feet, contains actual engines, fuel pumps, and early rocket models developed by the rocket pioneer in his workshop. The wing was financed, as in fact was much of his early research, by the Guggenheim Foundation. In the workshop there are shop sketches and blueprints, graphs, and the first motion picture record made in the United States of rocket firings.

In the words of one biographer, Dr. Goddard singlehandedly played a key role in developing rocketry from a vague dream into a significant branch of modern engineering. Although many of the artifacts and materials he used were crude by modern standards, his painstaking research and meticulously kept notebooks were truly landmarks in the early history of rocket technology.

Outside the Roswell Museum one may view his early launching tower, which was moved to the grounds of the museum in 1949. The rocket in it is an exact replica in size and shape of the last model he developed in the winter of 1941–1942 at Roswell.

Location: The Roswell Museum is at the corner of North Main Street and 11th Street in the downtown section of the city.

Schedule: Hours are from 9 a.m. to 5 p.m. daily and from 1 p.m. to 5 p.m. on Sundays and holidays. The museum is closed on Christmas Day and New Year's Day.

Admission: Free.

Missile Park Museum at White Sands Missile Range contains 37 rockets and missiles used by the U.S. Army, U.S. Navy, and U.S. Air Force. (Courtesy of the U.S. Army.)

White Sands Missile Park
White Sands, New Mexico

As a testing ground for new missiles, the White Sands Missile Range has been in use for almost 30 years. Even before the German V–2 rocket became operational near the end of World War II, the U.S. Army initiated a rocketry program. The first missile fired at White Sands was a Tiny Tim sounding rocket launched in September, 1945.

Since that time, the facility has been the testing site for almost all missiles developed by the U.S. Army, as well as for a number developed by the U.S. Navy, U.S. Air Force, and the National Aeronautics and Space Administration. The range covers a rectangle 100 miles long and 40 miles wide in the Tularosa Basin of south-central New Mexico and is the largest land area military installation in the United States.

Not all missiles have been fired within the limits of the missile range, for in the 1950s, various missiles were fired from points outside the state, subsequently impacting within the range.

An interesting point within the range area is Trinity Site, where the world's first atomic bomb was detonated on July 16, 1945. On the northern portion of the range, it is not open to the public since it is located within a missile impact area.

The Missile Park Museum was established in 1957 as part of an "open house" held at that time in conjunction with the installation's information program. It is entirely outdoors and covers an area of some 100,000 square feet. On display are a total of 37 missiles and rockets used by the U.S. Army, U.S. Air Force, and U.S. Navy, as well as a PEP (Planetary Entry Parachute) developed by NASA.

The Missile Park Museum is adjacent to the headquarters building of the Missile Range. Since it is located on a military installation, it is not open to the general public on a regular basis. Visitors may view the Missile Park Museum by appointment and may also photograph the exhibits by contacting the curator. The telephone number is (915) 678–1134.

Army rockets and missiles which are on display are a Nike-Ajax, Nike-Hercules, Nike-Zeus (now the Spartan), Redstone, Sergeant, Corporal, Pershing, Loon (U.S. version of the German V–1), V–2, WAC Corporal, Dart, SS–10, Honest John, Little John, Pogo Hi, Loki, an RP–76 target missile, Lark, XM–21 experimental ground-to-ground vehicle, Lacrosse, Shillelagh, Hawk, and "A" experimental anti-aircraft missile.

Air Force missiles are the Sidewinder, Mace, Athena, Falcon, Crossbow, Genie, Shavetail, and XQ drone target vehicle.

Navy missiles are the Terrier, Talos, Tarter, Aerobee Hi, and Aerobee 170.

Location: The White Sands Missile Range is located in south-central New Mexico between Alamogordo and Las Cruces. It is about 60 miles north of El Paso, Texas.

Schedule: Open during normal duty hours by appointment. See text above.

Admission: Free.

History of Aviation Collection
University of Texas
Austin, Texas

For more than half a century, there can have been very few connected with military aviation who haven't logged time over Texas. The nation's first military aircraft was shipped to Fort Sam Houston in February, 1910, where Lieutenant Benjamin D. Foulois made a total of 61 flights, teaching himself to fly with the assistance of an exchange of correspondence with the Wright brothers.

After only two years of service, Aeroplane No. 1 became a museum piece. It had taken such a heavy toll of damage that the War Department restored it and donated it to the Smithsonian Institution at the Wrights' suggestion.

From such beginnings, the role of Texas in military aviation had been assured. In later years the state was also to become important as a center of the aerospace industry, the manned space flight program, aerospace medicine, and airline operations.

By the early 1960s, an initiative leading toward the establishment of a history of aviation collection at the University of Texas was being considered. Then, in 1965, George Haddaway, longtime publisher and editor of *Flight Magazine*, offered his personal collection of aviation books and memorabilia to the university. From this nucleus, the History of Aviation Collection has grown to become the foremost such collection in the southwest.

This Glasflugel BS–1 sailplane was donated to the University of Texas Collection by Alvin H. Parker, a record-setting pilot who held several world distance titles. (Photo by Jay Miller.)

The collection's library alone numbers close to 8000 books, an additional 5000 miscellaneous bound volumes, 5000 photographs, and more than 100 personal albums of well-known aviators. Among the latter are those of the late Frank Hawks, along with many of his personal papers, and the personal files of the late Lewis Yancey.

Other notables in aviation who have contributed personal papers and memorabilia to the expanding collection include William G. Fuller, Dr. Ronald O. Stearman, Miss Viola Gentry, Dr. Warren Roberts, Alvin H . Parker, Miss Tony Page, and Selig Altschul.

The History of Aviation Collection occupies two rooms in the university's Academic Center, with a total of 2300 square feet, of which 900 square feet is devoted to exhibits. There is a full-time curator, himself an aviation historian and journalist.

A prominent place in the display area is occupied by two sailplanes: a Glasflugel BS–1, one of only 18 which were built; and a Sisu 1A, one of 10, in which Alvin H. Parker of Odessa, Texas set two sailplane distance records.

Glass cases contain a collection of some 500 scale models which were built by Phil Spexarth of Dallas, covering the history of aviation from 1903 to the present day.

Several engines are also exhibited: a 1918 Gnome Rhone Jb rotary engine, a Curtiss OX–5, a Guiberson A–1020 diesel engine, and two Continental O–470 engines. Numerous photographs, paintings, maps, instruments, propellors, controls, insigne, and other artifacts can also be seen.

The collection has some 20,000 back issues of magazines available to researchers. In fact, the principal emphasis in the development and availability of the collection has been as a research center which has attracted aviation historians from throughout the U.S. and abroad. The collection continues to actively solicit contributions of material and is entirely dependent upon donations in furthering its accessions program. Its relationship with the University of Texas provides an academic emphasis and long-term assurance of adequate facilities and support.

For serious researchers, the library section offers both a comprehensive and professionally catalogued resource, but even to the casual visitor to Austin the History of Aviation Collection is a fascinating slice of the heritage of flight.

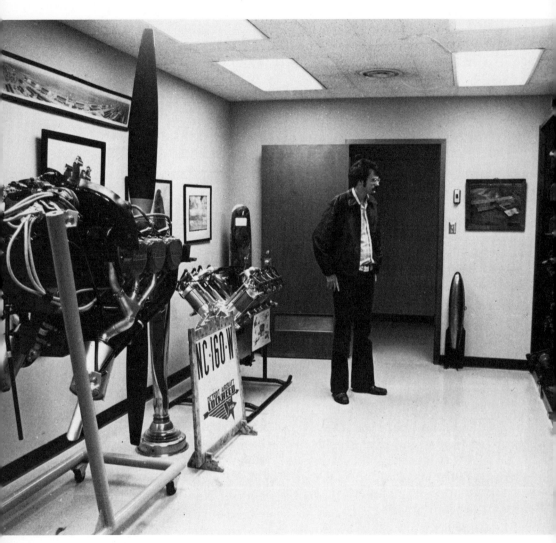

Engines, propellor blades, more than 500 scale models, a comprehensive collection of memorabilia, and a library makes the History of Aviation Collection a first-rate research resource. (Photo by Jay Miller.)

Location: The History of Aviation Collection is housed in Rooms 19 and 20 of the University of Texas Academic Center. The campus is in the northern part of Austin, bounded by Interstate Highway 35, 19th Street, Guadalupe Street, and 26th Street. Parking space is limited.

Schedule: Open Monday through Friday from 8 a.m. to 5 p.m., except during lunch. Can be opened on weekends by special arrangement. Telephone: (512) 471–4663.

Admission: Free.

Nine military aircraft stand outside the Pate Museum of Transportation and a pair of OH–21B helicopters stand on either side of the entrance. (Photo by Jon Allen.)

Pate Museum of Transportation
Fort Worth, Texas

A fourteen-mile drive south from Fort Worth takes one through gently rolling countryside along a highway flanked by cattle ranches and recreation areas with names like Mustang Park.

It's an attractive drive and well worth it, for the Pate Museum of Transportation is more than a pleasant reward. This remarkably diverse, well-maintained museum has been open since August, 1969, and its outdoor aircraft exhibit alone is well worth seeing.

There's even a London double-decker bus parked near the museum entrance, a private railway car, and a 54-foot minesweeper. The entrance to the building is flanked by two OH–21B helicopters.

The museum has a comfortable library and reading room with some 1500 volumes and a substantial collection of magazines, photographs, clippings, and models. In this room is a six-foot high model of a lunar module and a case containing the space suit in which Astronaut Alan Shepard walked on the moon.

In the main part of the building, in addition to some 35 automobiles exhibited, there are several aircraft models and a mockup of a Mercury capsule, as well as a 1930 Pietenpol Air Camper in excellent condition.

A small annex to the 9000-square-foot main building houses

The excellent library and reading room at the Pate Museum contains models, mock-ups, and Astronaut Alan Shepard's space suit. (Photo by Jon Allen.)

the museum's aircraft engine display. In the center of the room is a mammoth Pratt & Whitney RL20 engine, with 250,000 pounds of thrust. Nearby is a German jet engine, one of the first to be developed, which stands in front of a series of wall panels on the history of ballooning. Other displays on the history of aviation cover the experiments of Octave Chanute, the Wright Brothers, and others, and the development of military aviation in World War I.

The aircraft displayed outdoors are all military aircraft and include the C–47 and C–119 transports and CH–23B helicopter. Also on display are an HU–16B amphibian, a T–33, an F–101, an F–84, an F–86, and an F9F with wings folded as in carrier operations.

The Pate Museum of Transportation is maintained by the Pate Foundation, Inc. of Fort Worth and has been visited by people from throughout the U.S., as well as from abroad. Several of the aviation and space exhibits are on loan from the National Aeronautics and Space Administration and from the U.S. Air Force Museum.

Aircraft are not fenced in and visitors can walk around each of them. The museum's attractive setting within a large recreation area makes it a pleasant place to spend several hours, with something to occupy every member of the family.

Location: The Pate Museum of Transportation is 14 miles south of Fort Worth on Route 377. Exhibits are easily visible from the highway and signs identify the museum entrance. Ample free parking is available.

Schedule: Open daily except Monday from 9 a.m. to 5 p.m. Closed Christmas Day. Groups should make advance arrangements. Telephone (817) 332–1161.

Admission: Free.

The indoor museum of the Confederate Air Force contains World War II memorabilia, uniforms, guns, photographs, and equipment used by every branch of the armed forces. (Courtesy of the Confederate Air Force Museum.)

Confederate Air Force Flying Museum Harlingen, Texas

Anyone who has stood on the airport ramp at Harlingen, Texas and seen and heard the Ghost Squadron perform would be hard put not to agree that the Confederate Air Force Flying Museum generates a unique excitement all its own.

This amazing organization grew out of what was at first a purely informal flying fraternity of former military pilots who found 20 years ago that few surplus combat aircraft were on the market. Despite the fact that 300,000 warplanes were built in the U.S. during World War II, there had been little effort to preserve any in flying condition in the postwar years.

The original members of the Confederate Air Force started with a North American P–51 Mustang and a Grumman F8F Bearcat, based on a 2900-foot strip at Mercedes, Texas, in the lower Rio Grande Valley. They decided to acquire additional aircraft and banded together under the leadership of Lloyd Nolen, a former World War II flying instructor, to form the Confederate Air Force. The organization was chartered as a non-profit Texas corporation in September, 1961.

Today the unit has more than 1200 members, all of them holding the rank of colonel. Due to increasing national interest and the growth of the organization, four chapters have been established: a Gulf Coast Wing in Galveston; a New Mexico Wing in Hobbs; a Southern Minnesota Wing in Minneapolis; and a Dallas–Fort Worth Wing in Fort Worth.

The Ghost Squadron of the Confederate Air Force maintains more than 50 aircraft in flying condition. The organization has an indoor museum and two hangars. (Courtesy of the Confederate Air Force Museum.)

Although the organization is directed by a nine-member general staff, command of the Air Force is exercised by the mythical Colonel Jethro E. Culpepper who terms the unit a band of rebels in the sense they are "rebels with a cause," namely that the planes they preserve should never be forgotten or destroyed.

The purposes of the Air Force are to preserve *in flying condition* combat aircraft of all military services of the United States in World War II and to perpetuate the spirit in which the planes were flown for the defense of the nation.

During the first few years, the primary emphasis was on acquiring fighter aircraft, and by 1963 nine aircraft had been acquired. These were the P–38 Lightning, P–40 Warhawk, P–51D Mustang, F4F Wildcat, F6F Hellcat, F8F Bearcat, F4U Corsair, P–39 Aircobra, P–63 Kingcobra, and P–47 Thunderbolt.

Some aircraft could not be found in the United States, such as the P–63 and P–47, which were acquired from Honduras and Nicaragua respectively. Subsequently, aircraft of other nations were also added, including four Messerschmitt ME–109s, a Messerschmitt ME–108, a DeHaviland MK–35 Mosquito, and two Spitfire MK IXs.

By 1964, Confederate Air Force officers had started showing interest in light and medium bombers. First to arrive were the Douglas A–20 Havoc and Martin B–26 Marauder, and a First Bomb Wing was organized.

With an already comprehensive collection of aircraft in flying condition, the organization started its well-known air shows and traveled to perform at military bases in Ohio, Texas, and Florida, as well as at Rebel Field. With the collection having outgrown quarters at Mercedes, the Confederate Air Force moved to Harlingen in 1965 at the invitation of the city.

Present facilities used by the organization include three large hangars and an office building with combined floor space of more than 76,000 square feet. The office building houses an indoor museum and officers' club, and quarters for visiting members have been added to house them while staying at Rebel Field.

The indoor museum is open every day of the year and is divided into three sections, one each for the U.S. Army Air

Lockheed P-38 "Lightning," Messerschmitt BF109, and North American P–51 "Mustang" are among the aircraft participating in Confederate Air Force aerial shows. (Courtesy of the Confederate Air Force Museum.)

Corps, the U.S. Navy, and the Confederate Air Force's own archives and displays. A considerable amount of memorabilia, maps, guns, photographs, fuselage sections, and other items of interest are displayed. Both the fighter and bomber hangars are also open to the public when the unit is not flying, while the third hangar is used for maintenance. Larger aircraft are on static display outside on the 40 acres of ramp space used by the organization.

Today the Ghost Squadron consists of more than 50 aircraft and plans for future growth include an additional building. The unit puts on air shows regularly, continues to seek members, and seeks support for the expensive task of maintaining and flying its aircraft.

Aircraft which are in the collection include a B–17 Flying Fortress, B–24 Liberator, B–25 Mitchell (3 each); B–26 Marauder, A–20 Havoc, A–26 Invader (2 each); Lockheed Hudson, B–29 Superfortress, P–38 Lightning, P–51D Mustang (2 each); P–51C Mustang: P–39 Aircobra, P–40 Warhawk, P–47 Thunderbolt (7 each); and a P–63 Kingcobra.

Also included are an FG1D Corsair, FM2 Wildcat, F6F Hellcat, F8F Bearcat, F–82 Twin Mustang, Messerschmitt ME–109 (4 each); Spitfire MK IX (2 each); SB2C Helldiver, DeHavilland MK35 Mosquito, SBD Dauntless, TBM Avenger, PBY–5A Catalina, C–47 Skytrain, Messerschmitt ME–108, C–45, T–6 Texan (2 each); BT–15 Vultee, PT–17 Stearman (2 each); PT–22 (2 each), PT–19, PT–26, Focke Wulf 44 Stiegletz, and Stinson L–5.

Several replicas which are displayed are a BT–VAL, Japanese dive bomber (2 each); a T–6 Kate, Japanese torpedo bomber; and T–6 Zero, Japanese fighter (5 each).

Location: The Confederate Air Force Museum is located at the Harlingen Industrial Airpark, northeast of the town. It can be reached from Route 77 on Morgan Boulevard. Harlingen is 24 miles north of Brownsville and the Mexican border, or 136 miles south of Corpus Christi. Parking is available.

Schedule: Open from 9 a.m. to 5 p.m. Monday through Saturday, and from 1 p.m. to 6 p.m. on Sundays and holidays. An air show is held during the month of October.

Admission: $2.00 for adults, $1.00 for children. Reduced rates are available for groups.

The exhibit hall in Building 1 is among the areas open to visitors at the Lyndon B. Johnson Space Center. (Courtesy of NASA.)

Lyndon B. Johnson Space Center
Houston, Texas

At the National Aeronautics and Space Administration's Manned Spacecraft Center, renamed in honor of the late President Lyndon B. Johnson in August, 1973, a total of five buildings are open to visitors. More than 50,000 square feet of display area are devoted to the story of the U.S. manned space program.

Of primary interest is Building 1, the Visitor Orientation Center, containing an 800-seat auditorium in which continuous programs of films and lectures are held throughout the day. The Center's museum and exhibit hall is also in the building.

The building was constructed in 1963 and an additional 14,000 square feet were added to the exhibit hall in 1968. The major contents of the building are the Faith VII Mercury capsule, Gemini V spacecraft, Apollo XVII spacecraft, a lunar rover vehicle, a Lunar Module LTA–8, a Skylab display, several samples of lunar rock, and an Apollo Lunar Science Experiments Package (ALSEP) which receives live information from the ALSEP instruments placed on the moon's surface. Numerous other artifacts related to space flight and the Apollo program moon landings are displayed in the exhibit hall and in other parts of the building.

One room in the Visitor Orientation Center has been set aside in honor of President Johnson and contains portraits of

The Lyndon B. Johnson Space Center near Houston is the location of the National Aeronautics and Space Administration's (NASA) control center for U.S. manned space flights. (Courtesy of NASA.)

the President, furniture from his White House years, the original U.S. copy of the Outer Space Treaty of 1967, and other memorabilia.

A Mercury Redstone launch vehicle and capsule, an Apollo Little Joe 2, and a mockup of the Apollo lunar module stand outside the Visitor Orientation Center.

A block from the Visitor Orientation Center is one of two cafeterias for NASA employees. Located in Building 3, it is open to the general public and also contains a souvenir and gift shop with many items related to the U.S. space program available.

Two other buildings which contain training facilities for U.S. astronauts are open to the public. One, the Mission Training and Simulation Facility in Building 5, contains the Gemini, Apollo, and Skylab training simulators. The second, in Building 29, is the Flight Acceleration Facility. The rotunda of the building houses the world's largest centrifuge as well as exhibits on the space shuttle program, astronauts' space suits, and the mobile quarantine facility which was used by the crew of Apollo XII upon their return to earth from the moon. They entered it on the *USS Hornet,* and it was then transferred to the Johnson Space Center.

Building 30, NASA's well-known Mission Control Center, is open to visitors during times of low activity and only to those on conducted tours. The lobby contains a number of artifacts and there is a visitor viewing room from which visitors may watch NASA personnel in the Mission Control Room during missions.

All buildings are well identified to enable visitors to make self-guided tours on foot. Advance reservations for small groups can be made by calling (713) 483–4321 or by writing to the Center's Special Events Office.

The Johnson Space Center has been in use since September, 1963. Although a manned space flight starts a thousand miles away and ends on the deck of a ship even more distant, the Center is the U.S. astronauts' link with earth from lift-off to splashdown. It is also the place where astronauts are trained in an area where they and their families live, and certainly the best place to see the artifacts and hardware which have played an important part in the U.S. space program.

Location: The Lyndon B. Johnson Space Center is about 25 miles south of Houston on the Gulf Freeway, Routes 75 and 45, then three miles east of those highways on NASA Road No. 1.

Schedule: Open from 9 a.m. to 4 p.m. seven days a week, except on national holidays.

Admission: Free.

The array of manned spacecraft and rocketry at the Lyndon B. Johnson Space Center covers the complete history of the U.S. space program. (Courtesy of NASA.)

Edward H. White II Memorial Museum
Brooks Air Force Base
San Antonio, Texas

What is now known as the Edward H. White II Memorial Museum had its beginnings in 1966 when the U.S. Air Force first decided to establish a Museum of Flight Medicine at Brooks Air Force Base in San Antonio. It was named for Colonel White, the astronaut, after the native of San Antonio lost his life at Cape Kennedy in January, 1967.

A substantial number of the museum's exhibits trace the development of aviation and space medicine during the last fifty years, and to these have been added items related to the U.S. space program and to Colonel White's own achievements. The collection, which also includes a number of larger items on loan from the U.S. Air Force Museum in Dayton, Ohio, is housed in Hangar 9, a historic structure which was completely restored by a group of local citizens in 1969.

Hangar 9 was constructed, along with 15 others, as a "temporary structure" in 1918 when the base was a World War I training center for the Air Service of the Army Signal Corps. It is now the only remaining World War I hangar in the U.S. and provides the museum with 7800 square feet of exhibit space. An excellent library on aviation and aerospace medicine and related subjects is also available to researchers.

Aviation medicine was born during the war in 1917 when the first large-scale training program for pilots revealed that there were more aircraft accidents due to human error than to

A Standard J–1 sits in the 7800 square feet of display space in Hangar 9 at Brooks Air Force Base. Instruments and aerospace medicine testing devices are displayed in front of the photo panels. (Courtesy of the U.S. Air Force.)

mechanical error. The following year, the Air Service Medical Research Laboratory was established at Hazelhurst Field in Mineola, N.Y., and determined that pilots' eyesight, sense of equilibrium, heart action, psychological responses, and physical functions should be well-coordinated. In 1926, the facility was moved to Brooks Field at San Antonio. It was relocated to Randolph Field in 1931, but returned to Brooks Air Force Base in 1959 to occupy a complex of new buildings which were later to be an important center for the training and evaluation of U.S. astronauts. The laboratory was renamed the School of Aerospace Medicine in 1961, the same year that the last plane was flown from Brooks Air Force base and the flight line permanently closed.

Among items related to the history of aviation medicine which may be seen in the hangar are the original Barany Chair, first used in 1918 to test the equilibrium of student pilots, and an early low-pressure chamber used at Mitchell Field, N.Y. in 1918 and during the 1920s and 1930s at Wright Field, Ohio. Beside the latter stands the first space cabin simulator, designed by Dr. Hubertus Strughold, the acknowledged "father of aerospace medicine."

A model of the dynamic environmental simulator used at Wright-Patterson Air Force Base, as well as a rotational flight simulator used during the early training of astronauts for the U.S. space program, may also be viewed.

Standing in the center of the hangar is a Standard J–1 aircraft of the type used to train primary flight students at Brooks Field in 1918. It is on permanent loan from the U.S. Air Force Museum.

Nearby is a mockup of the Gemini IV module which served as a ground trainer for Colonel White and other astronauts prior to the space flight in Gemini IV during which Colonel White became the first man to "walk" in space. On June 2, 1965, he took a 20-minute trip outside the spacecraft, using a jet gun to propel himself. On that trip, he also carried the Air Force wings from the uniform of his father, a retired Air Force general, which were subsequently mounted and may be seen among Colonel White's memorabilia and decorations in the display cabinets in the museum.

A number of aircraft engines and propellors are also exhibited, including OX–5, Liberty, and K–12 engines, as well

Hangar 9 at Brooks Air Force Base houses the Edward H. White II Memorial Museum. Built in 1918 as a "temporary structure," it was restored in 1969 and is the only remaining World War I hangar in the United States. (Courtesy of the U.S. Air Force.)

as propellors from JN–4 and DH–4 aircraft.

The "man in space" section of the museum includes various examples of equipment used in space, as well as a collection of models. Samples of foods used by U.S. astronauts, a dental kit, and the zero gravity toilet developed by the School of Aerospace Medicine for the Skylab program may be seen.

One exhibit which has no connection with aviation or space, but which is valued highly by the museum, is a rostrum which has only been used twice. On the day before his assassination in Dallas on November 22, 1963, President John F. Kennedy dedicated the new School of Aerospace Medicine at Brooks Air Force Base and gave his last public address from the rostrum.

The second time it was used was on June 16, 1965, when Astronaut Colonel Edward H. White II spoke at Brooks Air Force Base. Six months later, he lost his life at Cape Kennedy. Since President Kennedy and Colonel White were the only two people ever to use the rostrum, it was decided to make it a permanent part of the museum's collection.

Location: The Edward H. White II Memorial Museum is located in Hangar 9, which was built as a "temporary structure" in 1918 at Brooks Air Force Base. The base is situated just off Southeast Military Drive in San Antonio and there are yellow directional signs to guide visitors to Hangar 9. Parking is available.

Schedule: Open Monday through Friday from 8 a.m. to 4:30 p.m. Closed on weekends and holidays.

Admission: Free.

The U.S. Air Force History and Traditions Museum at Lackland AFB, which opened in 1966, hosts 100,000 visitors a year. Lackland AFB is the home of the U.S. Air Force's basic military and officer training, so the museum also serves to acquaint Air Force men and women with the Air Force's role in national defense. (Courtesy of the U.S. Air Force.)

USAF History and Traditions Museum
Lackland Air Force Base
San Antonio, Texas

Hundreds of thousands of young men have received their first introduction to the U.S. Air Force upon arriving at San Antonio, Texas, to enter training at Lackland Air Force Base. For more than a generation, it has provided basic military training, officer training, or aviation cadet pre-flight training at various times.

It's a busy installation today, but nowhere as busy as it was in the first months of the Korean Conflict when as many as 67,000 men enlisted in the Air Force and entered basic training in a single month. A good many men still in the Air Force, and even some who have retired, recall, with a distinct lack of nostalgia, the time when some 19,000 trainees slept in tents because of overcrowded barracks.

At that time, the Air Force was adding to its history and still developing traditions. Fifteen more years remained before it was decided to establish a museum on the base which would serve primarily as an extension of the base's training role in preparing airmen and officers for service in the Air Force.

Today, the museum draws 100,000 visitors a year. Its 9600 square feet of exhibit space are used to display items of significance to the evolution of aviation and to the growth of the U.S. Air Force. The History and Traditions Museum also contains a small reference library and archives with books, periodicals, photographs, news articles, documents, aircraft

The Museum's P–51H–5 North American Mustang carries the markings of the 487th Fighter Squadron and of Major John C. Meyer who is now a general and commander-in-chief of the Strategic Air Command. (Courtesy of the U.S. Air Force.)

records, and technical data. Although many of the visitors are military personnel stationed at Lackland AFB and other nearby installations, the museum is open to the public without charge and there are regular film showings scheduled at 10 a.m. and 2 p.m. every day.

Inside the museum there are a number of three-dimensional dioramas depicting early aviation scenes such as Civil War and World War I ballooning. More modern warfare is illustrated with some of the major air battles of World War II. Numerous instruments, gun turrets, weapons, and other artifacts are exhibited, as is a restored Curtiss JN–4 Jenny without fabric covering.

The museum contains some 15 aircraft engines, ranging from a 1909 Gnome nine-cylinder rotary engine to a 1947 Marquardt XFJ 31–MA–1 ramjet of 1946. Others which may be seen, all of which are restored in excellent condition, are a Curtiss OX–5 which powered the Jenny and other aircraft; a LeRhone rotary, built in the U.S. by Union Switch and Signal Co., which powered the Nieuport, Caudron, Standard E–1, and others; a 12-cylinder Liberty engine which powered many pre-World War II aircraft and was even used in British and Soviet tanks during World War II; a 1919 Hispano-Suiza which was used in the Spad; a Lawrence L4; a Wright J–5C Whirlwind; a Wright R–1820 Cyclone used on the B–17 Flying Fortress; a Packard DR–980; an Allison V–1710–143–145 used in the P–38, P–39, P–40, and P–51 aircraft; a Pratt & Whitney R–1830–65 Twin Wasp; a Pratt & Whitney R–4360–43 Wasp Major, used on the B–36 and B–50; a General Electric-Allison J–33 turbojet used on the F–84B and F–89 aircraft.

There are a total of 45 aircraft and missiles on static display outside the museum. Not all are adjacent to the building, but are located at various sites on the base; however, they are part of the museum's collection and a folder is available at the museum listing the displays and indicating their locations.

A number of duplicate aircraft are shown, but the principal types are readily divided into fighters, bombers, trainers, cargo aircraft, and missiles. there is one rescue aircraft, a Grumman HU–16B Albatross, and one helicopter, a Sikorsky H–19B Chickasaw.

Fighter aircraft on display are a Republic P–47N Thunder-

Three-dimensional diorama in the History and Traditions Museum shows a World War I observation balloon being prepared by the ground crew to carry two observers aloft. (Courtesy of the U.S. Air Force.)

bolt, a North American F–51H Mustang, a Bell P–63 King Cobra, two Lockheed F–80A Shooting Stars, a North American F–82 Twin Mustang, two Republic F–84 Thunderjets (B and C models), four Republic F–84F Thunderstreaks, a North American EF–86A Sabrejet, a Northrop EF–89A Scorpion, a Lockheed YF–94A Starfire, six North American GF–100A Super Sabrejets, a McDonnell TF–101F Voodoo, three Convair F–102A Delta Daggers, a Lockheed F–104C Starchief, and two Republic F–105B Thunderchiefs.

The bombers are a Douglas TB–17G Flying Fortress, a Ford EB–24M Liberator, and a Martin RB–57A Canberra. Cargo aircraft are a Beech UC–45J Expeditor, a Douglas C–47D Skytrain, and a Fairchild C–119C Flying Boxcar. Trainers include two Lockheed T–33A Shooting Stars, a Cessna XT–37 Tweetybird, and a Northrop T–38A Talon.

Missiles which are displayed are the Ryan Firebird, two Boeing Bomarcs, two Republic Loons, a Martin Mace, a Martin Matador, a McDonnell Quail, and a Douglas Thor.

Location: The Air Force History and Traditions Museum is on Orville Wright Drive, west of the main entrance to Lackland Air Force Base. Lackland may be reached on Interstate 410, Route 90W, or Southwest Military Highway (Route 13).

Schedule: Open Monday through Friday from 7:30 a.m. to 4 p.m. and on Saturdays, Sundays, and holidays from 9 a.m. to 6 p.m. Closed on Christmas Day.

Admission: Free.

WEST

Science of Aviation exhibit occupies most of the second floor of the Museum of Science and Industry. The separate Space Museum is in a building across the street. (Photo by Jon Allen.)

Museum of Science and Industry
Los Angeles, California

The California Museum of Science and Industry is one of the state's leading educational facilities, with more than two dozen permanent exhibit halls in a spacious three-story building. There are exhibits on electricity, communications, energy, health, parks and forests, agriculture, and other subjects. Each is designed and constructed as an educational unit and the museum is usually crowded with youngsters.

The museum has three sections containing aviation and space related material which are integrated into the museum's permanent exhibits. While none is distinctive or unusual, they are the only such exhibits within the city proper.

The largest such section is the Science of Aviation Exhibit, occupying most of the main building's second floor. Here there are displays on airframe construction, the earth's atmosphere, airfoils, helicopters, navigation, earth orbits, and jet, rocket, and internal combustion engines. The story of flight is told through paintings and photos of the history of ballooning, aviation and rocket pioneers, with a number of working exhibits equipped with earphones.

Many of the displays are provided by companies prominent in the Southern California aerospace industry and credits are given by the museum to firms such as Aerojet General, Douglas, Hughes Aircraft, Lockheed California, North American Aviation, the Northrop Corporation, and Pratt & Whitney.

Lockheed sponsors a scale model showing the interior and exterior of the L–1011 Tristar, with a continuous color film which traces the story of the aircraft's development.

On the museum's main floor, glass cases in the hallway contain scale models of more than 100 aircraft, divided into three sections: military, commercial, and experimental. A special exhibit on Air Traffic Control, sponsored by the Federal Aviation Administration, may be seen nearby.

Across State Drive from the main museum building, a Thor-Agena missile marks the entrance to the building in which a separate Space Museum is housed. Here there are several exhibits provided by industry and the Air Force, as well as a National Aeronautics and Space Administration display complete with mock-up of a Mariner IV satellite. A small environmental sciences laboratory may also be seen.

Location: The California Museum of Science and Industry is on State Drive in Exposition Park, near the intersection of Exposition Boulevard and Figueroa Street. It can be reached easily on the half a dozen freeways which converge near downtown Los Angeles. The museum buildings have ample parking space available and are situated close to the Coliseum and the University of Southern California campus.

Schedule: Daily from 10 a.m. to 5 p.m.

Admission: Free.

The National Aeronautics and Space Administration and southern California space firms have provided exhibits for the Museum of Science and Industry's space exhibit. (Photo by Jon Allen.)

Point Mugu Missile Park
Point Mugu, California

Point Mugu, California, is the U.S. Navy's principal missile development and testing center and the headquarters location for the Naval Missile Center and the Pacific Missile Range. A number of other Navy organizations are also located on the 4600-acre base, including the Navy Astronautics Group, which operates and maintains the Navy's space and satellite systems, and the test squadron which evaluates airborne weapons systems.

The Naval Missile Center was first established at Point Mugu in 1946 and most U.S. Navy missiles have been tested on the range which stretches far into the Pacific Ocean. The range also serves the other armed services, NASA, and other government agencies. It has both land-based tracking stations in the Pacific and ships and aircraft under its control.

For visitors to the base or motorists traveling the Pacific Coast Highway, the base established a small missile park just outside the main gates several years ago. The 11 missiles on display, which are maintained in excellent condition, are fairly representative of the weapons which have been developed and tested at Point Mugu.

Since the park is outside the installation proper, it is readily visible. The missiles displayed in it are the Bullpup A, Bullpup B, Hawk, Lark, Oriole, Sidewinder, Sparrow I, Sparrow III, Regulus I, Regulus II, and Polaris A1.

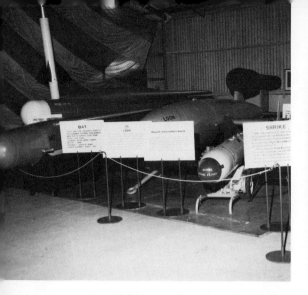

In addition to the outside exhibit, some two dozen U.S. Navy missiles may be seen by tour groups in the briefing building at Point Mugu. (Courtesy of the U.S. Navy.)

Eleven U.S. Navy missiles are exhibited in a small park near the entrance to the Naval Missile Center at Point Mugu, headquarters of the Pacific Missile Range. (Courtesy of the U.S. Navy.)

The Pacific Missile Range headquarters also conducts a tour program for groups as part of its community relations program, but prior arrangements with the public affairs office are necessary.

As part of the briefing and tour, groups visit Building 363 which contains some two dozen missiles and targets, either full-size or in scale models. Missile hardware which is in the Navy inventory, but which is on loan to other museums in California, numbers an additional 20 or so.

The missiles which can be seen by tour groups are mostly smaller in size than those exhibited outside. They include a Bat, Petrel, Corvus, Bullpup A, Bullpup B, Sidewinder 1A, Sidewinder 1C, Sparrow I, Sparrow II, Sparrow III, MQM–36A, Oriole, Talos model, AQM–37A, Sparoair, Sidewinder ARCAS, Loon, Phoenix, Shrike, KDA, Walleye, and additional test models and aerial rockets.

Location: Point Mugu is located on the Pacific Coast Highway just south of Oxnard, California. The base missile park is visible from the highway adjacent to gate no. 2.

Schedule: The missile park may be viewed year-round. Visits to the missile display building and briefings on the mission of the base may be scheduled by groups making written arrangements with the public affairs office in advance.

Admission: Free.

International Aerospace Hall of Fame San Diego, California

A walk through the International Aerospace Hall of Fame gives a visitor a chronological insight into the achievements of close to 50 individuals whose contributions to aviation and space technology have been recognized by the organization.

The entry hall, decorated with wing ribs and propellors, is filled with photographs of early flight. At a central kiosk, an automatic projection system is used to introduce visitors to the history of aviation and space flight. The film which is shown, *Those We Honor,* was produced by the Hall of Fame's Heritage for Youth Program and is available free of charge to schools throughout the world. Its costs are entirely supported by donations and membership fees in the International Aerospace Hall of Fame.

An oil painting of each of the honorees hangs in the Hall of Fame, along with a plaque describing his or her life and achievements. Artifacts which are related to each of the honorees are exhibited in display cases throughout the hall.

In addition to the memorabilia displayed, the Hall of Fame also maintains an excellent library and research facility containing numerous books, early photographs, and documents. This material is available to researchers and historians and additions are actively sought in keeping with the organization's objective of preserving historical material.

Those who have been honored by the Hall of Fame include

military figures, aviation pioneers, scientists, designers, and astronauts. Among the latter are Neil A. Armstrong, Michael Collins, John H. Glenn, Jr., Walter M. Schirra, and Alan B. Shepard. Russian Cosmonaut Yuri A. Gagarin, first man to orbit the earth, is also honored.

Early pioneers and designers include Glenn H. Curtiss, Reuben H. Fleet, Louis Bleriot, Geoffrey de Havilland, Roy R. Grumman, Fred H. Rohr, T. Claude Ryan, and John K. Northrop.

Also honored are the Wright Brothers, Alberto Santos-Dumont, Air Commodore Frank Whittle, Otto Lilienthal, Igor Sikorsky, Major General William E. Mitchell, Dr. Robert H. Goddard, Donald W. Douglas, and Anthony Fokker.

Military figures include Air Marshal William A. Bishop of Canada, Edward V. Rickenbacker, Manfred von Richtofen, Admiral John H. Towers, Rear Admiral Richard E. Byrd, and Lieutenant General James H. Doolittle. The women named to the Hall of Fame are Amelia Earhart and Jacqueline Cochran.

The International Aerospace Hall of Fame was founded in 1964 and is administered by a board of directors composed of

Close to fifty portraits of those who have been honored by the International Aerospace Hall of Fame are surrounded by memorabilia illustrating early aviation history. (Courtesy of the International Aerospace Hall of Fame.)

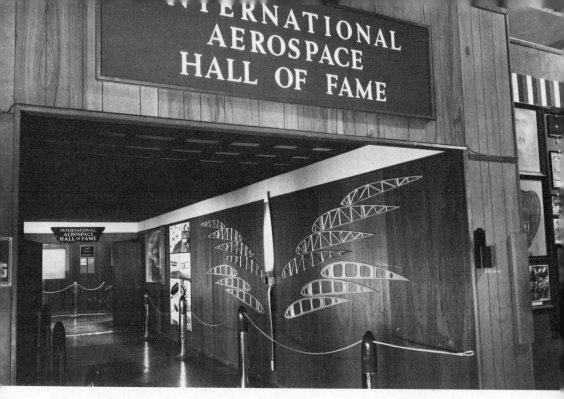

The International Aerospace Hall of Fame is located in San Diego's Balboa Park and shares space with the San Diego Aerospace Museum. (Courtesy of the International Aerospace Hall of Fame.)

residents of the San Diego area. Nominations for individuals to be honored by the Hall of Fame are made by a board of electors comprised of 125 persons prominent in aviation and space activities. About half of the electors are non-U.S. citizens.

Much of the organization's present emphasis is on educational activities, with school programs designed both to inform groups visiting the Hall of Fame and to carry the purposes of the Hall of Fame to schools through educational materials.

The Hall of Fame is co-located with the San Diego Aerospace Museum in the city's Balboa Park, although it is administered and directed as a separate organization.

Location: The International Aerospace Hall of Fame is located in Balboa Park, in the same building as the San Diego Aerospace Museum. It can be reached on Park Boulevard or Sixth Avenue to El Prado.

Schedule: Open daily from 10 a.m. to 4:30 p.m., except on Thanksgiving Day, Christmas Day, and New Year's Day.

Admission: Free.

The replica of Charles A. Lindbergh's *Spirit of St. Louis* in the San Diego Aerospace Museum flew in the Paris Air Show in 1967. The original Lindbergh aircraft, a Ryan monoplane was designed and built in San Diego. (Courtesy of the San Diego Aerospace Museum.)

San Diego Aerospace Museum
San Diego, California

The San Diego Aerospace Museum is one of seven local museums in the city, of which six are located in Balboa Park, among them San Diego's famous zoo. It was opened to the public in February, 1963, and since 1965 has been housed in a temporary exposition building in which it shares space with the city's Hall of Science museum. The Aerospace Museum is second only to the zoo in popularity with visitors, who now number close to one million every year.

The purpose of the museum has been to illustrate the story of the long involvement of San Diego in the early days of aviation and the growth of the aerospace industry. Several major firms are located in or near the city, and as early as 1911 it drew Glenn H. Curtiss there for some of his early flights and drew military aviators to the stations at the U.S. Navy's North Island and the U.S. Army's Rockwell Field at Coronado. The city's airport, in fact, was named in honor of Charles A. Lindbergh in 1928, the only airport so named.

Lindbergh's *Spirit of St. Louis* was designed and built in San Diego by the Ryan Aeronautical Company, and a bust of the transatlantic solo aviator which was presented by the firm is on permanent display in the airport terminal's passenger concourse.

The museum's contents are divided into three sections, one covering general aviation and early pioneers, another on

armed forces aviation, and a third, in cooperation with the
National Aeronautics and Space Administration, on modern
space flight.

An integral part of the museum is its historical library and
archives, which is one of the best in the country. Containing
vintage aeronautical books, manuals, photographs, and
numerous documents, it is named in honor of two pioneering
brothers, Earl D. Prudden and George A. Prudden, who
played important roles in the growth of the city's aerospace
industry, and it has been provided with an endowment to
maintain and expand the collection.

That the museum is among the best of its size and type in
the country and that the numerous volunteers who have
helped to restore aircraft and staff the museum and its gift
shop have done a worthy job was confirmed by Lindbergh
himself when he visited the museum in 1972.

The museum's general aviation section contains a flying
replica of the first seaplane built in the United States, Curtiss'
A–1, which was flown in San Diego and sold to the U.S. Navy.
Also in this section is a reproduction of the Wright Brothers'
first aircraft, as well as a Chanute 1909 glider, a Montgomery
1911 monoplane, and a Bowlus glider.

In the center of the general aviation section is a flying
reproduction of Lindbergh's *Spirit of St. Louis* which
re-enacted the last 20 miles of his flight to Paris on May 21,
1967, and appeared at the Paris Air Show that year. This
aircraft has also been used for the filming of television
documentary programs. Another Ryan aircraft of 1927 on
display is the M–1, the first production monoplane produced
in the United States.

Additional items of interest are the Chana Wee Bee, the
world's smallest aircraft, as well as several dozen engines
from early pistons to jets and propellors and accessories.

The armed forces section contains both Air Force and Navy
planes, including a Grumman F9F Panther which was flown
by the Navy's precision aerobatic team, The Blue Angels.
There is also a Curtiss P–40N Warhawk of World War II.
Other aircraft on display include a Lockheed T–33 trainer, a
Sikorsky HH–19G helicopter, and an XV–5A Vertifan vertical
take-off aircraft mockup.

The space flight section consists of a regular series of

displays provided by NASA. There is a Mercury capsule, scale models of the Gemini, Apollo, and Lunar Module craft, as well as communications satellites and astronauts' equipment.

The Aerospace Museum also owns a number of aircraft which need to be restored and these are mostly stored at Lindbergh Field. During 1974, the 30 restoration volunteers were working on three aircraft which will be added to the permanent exhibits when they are completed. These are a Curtiss JN–4D Jenny, built in 1916; a Ryan SCE of 1938; and a Japanese Mitsubishi A6M5 Zero which was recovered from Rabaul Harbour in 1971.

Membership in the San Diego Aerospace Museum is open

This 1961 reproduction of a 1911 Curtiss A–1, first U.S. seaplane and first aircraft purchased by the U.S. Navy, is still in flying condition. (Courtesy of the San Diego Aerospace Museum.)

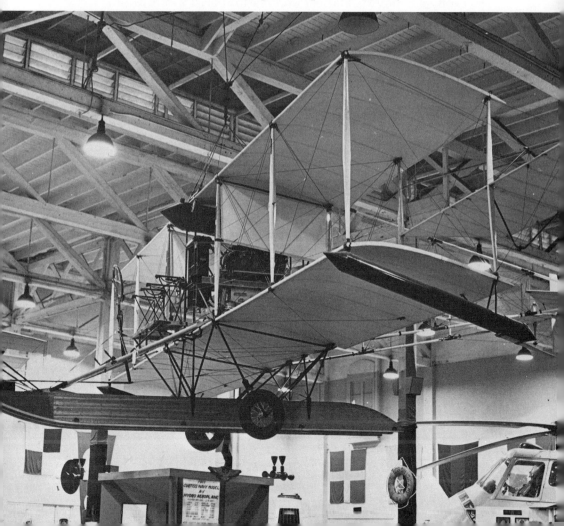

to anyone interested in its activities and the membership dues help to support its work. The annual membership fee includes a subscription to the museum's quarterly publication, *Countdown,* and to a monthly newsletter which was started in November, 1973, entitled *Wings and Things.*

The museum also maintains an aviation pioneers logbook, a register for people connected with aviation prior to 1940, which is kept in the Prudden Historical Library and Archives. Late in 1973 the museum acquired a unique collection of aviation trophies, artifacts, and memorabilia belonging to the late aviatrix Gladys Berry O'Donnell, who later became prominent in politics.

Location: The San Diego Aerospace Museum is in San Diego's Balboa Park, between Park Boulevard and Sixth Avenue. It can be reached on El Prado, midway between the city's Fine Arts Gallery and Natural History Museum.

Schedule: Open daily from 10 a.m. to 4:30 p.m., except on Thanksgiving Day, Christmas Day, and New Year's Day.

Admission: Free.

Movieland of the Air
Santa Ana, California

If a visitor to Movieland of the Air has a feeling of already having seen many of the more than 20 aircraft on display in the museum's attractive 50,000 square foot building, he's absolutely right!

Millions of people have seen the aircraft before and will probably continue to recognize them on the Late Show.

As the name of the museum implies, Frank Tallman's $2 million collection of aircraft, motion picture props, memorabilia, and miscellany has been used in dozens of motion pictures and television programs.

For starters, some of the aircraft were used in *Tobruk, Catch–22, Tora! Tora! Tora!, A Yank in the RAF, Flying Tigers, Murphy's War,* and *The Court Martial of Billy Mitchell.*

In addition to combat roles, replicas of vintage aircraft and open-cockpit planes which starred in comedies and thrillers can be seen. Among these were *The Perils of Pauline, It's a Mad, Mad, Mad, Mad World, The Great Race, Darling Lili, Fate is the Hunter,* and *North by Northwest.*

An interesting facet of the way in which the aircraft are displayed is the use of photographs, posters, props, and costumes which were actually used in the films. There are even replicas of several old movie sets from such classics as *Hell's Angels, Catch–22,* and *Dawn Patrol.*

247

Curtiss P–40N Tomahawk is among the World War II combat aircraft used by Allies and Axis on display at Movieland of the Air. (Photo by Jon Allen.)

Equally as interesting as the museum is the story behind Tallmantz Aviation, which opened the museum in December, 1963. For many years previously, motion picture pilots Frank Tallman and Paul Mantz had dominated the flying assignments connected with Hollywood productions. Rather than remain competitors, they joined forces and formed their own company, based at Orange County Airport. With their associates, Frank Pine and Jim Appleby, both pilots, they handled motion picture assignments and took on an increasing number of television commercial flights. The firm's modified B–25 camera plane, which can be seen on the airport ramp, has been used for numerous air-to-air film sequences.

Mantz lost his life in the summer of 1965 in a tragic on-location accident during the filming of *The Flight of the Phoenix.* Tallman himself sustained minor injuries during an accident in 1973, but was back in the air and working on another motion picture early the following year.

Scattered among the aircraft in the museum are exhibits about various aspects of aviation, from ballooning to space flight. The story of the Powder–Puff Derby women's air race is illustrated, along with a section on women in aviation and photographs and articles about Amelia Earhart. Still photos from films and clippings tell the exploits and "roles" played by pilots Tallman, Mantz, Pine, and Appleby.

One display is devoted to precision flying teams such as the U.S. Navy's Blue Angels, the U.S. Air Force Thunderbirds, and the Royal Air Force Red Arrows.

A replica of the front of a World War I hangar bears the inscription "Lafayette Escadrille" and display cases are filled with memorabilia and more than a dozen machine guns of the period. A bookshelf is filled with Lindberghiana, copies of the Lone Eagle's books, and various mementos. At the rear of the museum, two sections are devoted to aircraft engines, of which there are more than two dozen exhibited, along with miscellaneous propellors and models.

Two sections of the museum hold special interest. One is the "Little Theatre" in which 16mm prints of feature films and aviation films are shown. The other section is a gallery of photographs—hundreds of pictures on military, commercial, and general aviation depicting pioneers, heroes, and innumerable unsung pilots who contributed to the history of aviation.

Many of the Movieland of the Air planes, it should be noted, are not authentic, and some are mockups which were built specifically for use in movies. However, the overall flavor of the museum's main display area is among the most intriguing in the country.

The grim-looking trio of Japanese warplanes—a Mitsubishi Zero, an Aichi D3A1 "Val," and a Nakajima "Kate"—are all "ringers" having been remodeled from U.S. aircraft such as a T–6, but they've fooled many a movie audience.

Other aircraft exhibited include a Grumman J2F–6 amphibian, a Curtiss JN–4 Jenny, a Waco UPF–7, a P-51B Mustang, a Curtiss P–40N Tomahawk, an S.E. 5a, and a Boeing F4B Navy biplane of 1928.

Movieland of the Air is housed in a modern building next to the Tallmantz Aviation hangar at the Orange County Airport. The collection contains more than two dozen vintage aircraft. (Photo by Jon Allen.)

This North American P–51B, raced by Paul Mantz, held numerous records. Aircraft in Movieland range from a replica of a Wright 1903 Flyer to planes used in World War II films. (Photo by Jon Allen.)

Also included is a 1918 U.S. Navy Orenco two-seat observation plane. Replicas and mock-ups include a Wright 1903 Flyer, a Sopwith Tripe, a Bleriot XI, a Borel-Morane of 1911, a Fokker DR–1 Triplane, and a 1910 Curtiss Pusher.

The museum has a small souvenir counter and lounge area, and soft drinks are available.

Location: Movieland of the Air is at the west end of the general aviation area at Orange County Airport. The airport is close to the junction of the Santa Ana Freeway and the Newport Freeway, about 40 miles southeast of Los Angeles.

Schedule: Open daily except Mondays from 10 a.m. to 6 p.m.

Admission: Adults, $1.75; ages 12 to 21, 75 cents; under 12 years of age, 50 cents.

Vintage aircraft and automobiles are part of the growing collection at Northwest Aero Museum. Biplane flight instruction, ballooning, and parachuting are all available at the "home of fun flying." (Photo by Jack Goins.)

Northwest Aero Museum
Henley Aerodrome
Coeur d'Alene, Idaho

A 1918 British aerodrome in the heart of Kootenai County, Idaho? Sure enough! Three miles south of Athol and 15 miles north of Coeur d'Alene, one can eat fish and chips at the Wingover Inn and watch the Tiger Moths, Nieuports, and Fokkers flash by!

When Clayton Henley left his native Kellogg, Idaho, to become an Air Force flight instructor during World War II, he always knew he'd return and that he would impart his love of flying to others.

The result is Henley Aerodrome and the emphasis is on the pleasure of flying. In fact Henley calls his operation "the home of fun flying" and he and his colleagues have created an atmosphere which makes a visit fun for everyone.

Henley Aerodrome is a popular location for fly-ins by groups such as the Antique Airplane Association and the Experimental Aircraft Association. Several airshows have been held there in the last couple of years and on summer weekends Henley and his colleagues have put on simulated World War I "dogfights" with their vintage squadron.

Flight instruction is the basic business at Henley Aerodrome and Henley is very much an advocate of the "stick and rudder" school of flying. Instruction in hot air ballooning is also available year-round from veteran aviatrix Gladys Buroker, and in 1973 a skydiving team was formed. The

Henley Aerodrome is a flying museum with emphasis on the World War I period. It is a popular location for antique and experimental aircraft fly-ins. (Photo by Jack Goins.)

10-man Henley Hummer group has participated in several competitions.

Facilities include two 60 × 70 foot hangars to house the collection of vintage and contemporary aircraft. A line of flagpoles flies the flags of half a dozen nations and Wingover Inn, a Tudor-style building designed by a young English friend of the Henleys, houses a souvenir counter and dining area. This is under the supervision of Mrs. Nadine Henley, herself a pilot.

In addition to a 2600-foot surfaced runway, a sod strip is used for the vintage aircraft. While Henley Aerodrome is in Idaho, it's only some 30 miles east of Spokane, Washington, which helped attract a record number of visitors during Expo 74. There's also a residential subdivision of 28 units on the property, with a motel scheduled for construction in the near future.

The aerodrome is decorated with World War I insigne and the Henleys have assembled a collection of artifacts which will be displayed with the aircraft. One can't count on all the aircraft being available for inspection during a visit, since Henley Aerodrome, like Old Rhinebeck, is a flying museum. The collection contains two DeHavilland Tiger Moths, a pair of Nieuport 24 replicas, and a Fokker Triplane for starters, with work underway on additional aircraft. Henley also has a couple of Piper J-3 Cubs and a Great Lakes Trainer, as well as modern aircraft used for flight instruction, charter work and other assignments.

Location: On Route 95, three miles south of Athol and 15 miles north of Coeur d'Alene, Idaho.

Schedule: Daylight hours during good weather.

Admission: Free.

Aircraft such as this Curtiss JN–4–D Jenny at Harrah's are all extremely well restored and are usually accompanied by explanatory displays. (Courtesy of Harrah's Automobile Collection.)

Harrah's Automobile Collection
Reno, Nevada

The quite incredible Harrah's Automobile Collection is a popular commercial attraction in Reno, primarily devoted to vintage cars. In among the estimated 1300 or more automobiles, however, enthusiasts will also find more than 60 motorcycles, 14 boats, and a 1906 San Francisco cable car. There's also a Pony Express Museum.

Not to be overlooked are the aircraft—eleven at last count. So anyone interested in seeing the latter will get more than their money's worth, with sufficient time to enjoy the other collections.

Bill Harrah, who operates hotels and casinos at Reno and Lake Tahoe, started collecting in 1948 with two automobiles. Today, he needs 13 buildings on a 10-acre complex to house the collection. A visitor can spend the entire day in the museum, which has a saloon and cafeteria on the premises, and in summer months, he needn't leave until 10 p.m.

Almost half of the aircraft in the collection are Curtiss products, starting with the Curtiss JN–4–D of 1918. Others are a Curtiss Robin B of 1928, a Curtiss Junior CW–1 of 1931, a Curtiss Fledgling of 1929, and a Curtiss P–40M fighter of 1943.

Other aircraft displayed are a Ford Tri-Motor 5 AT–B of 1928, the *City of Reno;* an Aeronca C–3 of 1937; an Arrow Sport Model F of 1937; a Travelair S–6000-B of 1929; and a

Monocoupe 90A of 1934. Bringing up the tail end is the most modern aircraft, a Lockheed P–38L fighter aircraft of 1945.

Location: Harrah's Automobile Collection is off Glendale Road, 3½ miles east of North Virginia Street. Motorists should take East 2nd Street, which becomes Glendale Road at Kietzke Lane. Free transportation is available from Harrah's Hotel in downtown Reno by vintage bus or 1906 San Francisco cable car, depending on the weather.

Schedule: Open daily from 9 a.m. to 10 p.m. from Memorial Day through Labor Day. Hours in winter are from 9 a.m. to 6 p.m.

Admission: $2.50 for adults; $1.00 for minors; children under 6 years admitted free. Family rates are available.

The 1928 Fort Tri-Motor *City of Reno* is the largest aircraft on display in the small aviation collection at Harrah's in Reno. (Courtesy of Harrah's Automobile Collection.)

Seattle Museum of History and Industry
Seattle, Washington

The aviation wing of the Seattle Museum of History and Industry bears the name of a remarkable man. Philip G. Johnson became president of the Boeing Airplane Company at the age of 31, and five years later when Boeing Air Transport, National Air Transport, Pacific Air Transport, and Varney Air Lines combined to form United Air Lines, he became its first president.

Johnson and his wife were early benefactors of the Seattle Historical Society. The dedication of the museum building in February, 1952, came eight years after his death, but it was appropriate that the museum's 2000-square-foot aviation wing bear his name, both because of his tireless role in guiding the growth of the Boeing Airplane Company, especially during World War II, and his strong personal interest in the museum.

In 1945, the year following Johnson's death, Boeing announced a gift of $50,000 to the museum for construction of the aviation wing.

The wing features much which traces the development of Boeing, not only in aviation since World War I, but also in the space age. The first aircraft acquired by the museum was a fully restored B–1 flying boat, built by Boeing in 1919. Acquired in 1942 and restored in 1951, it is the aircraft which was used by Eddie Hubbard to fly the first contract

Early airmail flights, airline history, and scale models of every aircraft built by the Boeing Airplane Company are among exhibits in the Philip G. Johnson wing. One display commemorates the first flight in Seattle on May 28, 1910. (Courtesy of the Boeing Company.)

The Seattle Museum of History and Industry is situated in McCurdy Park. In addition to the aviation wing, the museum also has an outstanding maritime collection and memorabilia connected with the development of the Pacific Northwest. (Courtesy of the Boeing Company.)

Boeing B–1, built in 1919, which flew airmail between Seattle and Victoria, B.C. for almost ten years, dominates the Philip G. Johnson Aviation Wing of the Seattle Museum of History and Industry. (Courtesy of the Boeing Company.)

international airmail service from the U.S. to Canada—between Seattle and Victoria, B.C. It remained in service for 10 years.

Also included are displays of models of all Boeing aircraft to the present day and of space projects in which the company has played a role: lunar orbiter, lunar rover, and the Saturn booster vehicle. There is an eight-foot lighted cutaway model of a Boeing 747 displayed beneath the B–1, which is suspended from the museum ceiling.

One display containing propellors, photographs, and other memorabilia commemorates Thomas F. Hamilton's first flight in Seattle on May 28, 1910. Since the opening of the museum, Boeing has assumed much of the responsibility for providing new exhibits and maintaining the collection, although there are a number of displays not devoted to the company, but dealing with the early aviation history of the Puget Sound area.

In addition to the aviation wing, the Seattle Museum of History and Industry also boasts an excellent maritime collection and a ground transportation wing containing horse-drawn vehicles, fire engines, and one of the city's first cable cars.

The museum maintains a library and its 500-seat auditorium is available to civic and non-profit organizations for meetings. A book shop and sales counter are also operated.

Location: The Museum of History and Industry is located in McCurdy Park at the end of East Hamlin Street, just south of the University of Washington Stadium and east of Montlake Boulevard. It may be reached by bus. Ample free parking is available.

Schedule: Open from 11 a.m. to 5 p.m. from Tuesday through Friday; 10 a.m. to 5 p.m. on Saturday; and noon to 5 p.m. on Sunday. Closed Christmas Day and New Year's Day.

Admission: Free.

CANADA

Reynolds Museum's 1929 Avro 594 Avian IV is one of seven aircraft displayed, most of which have seen service in Western Canada. Taxiway connects the museum to the local airport. (Courtesy of the Reynolds Museum.)

Reynolds Museum
Wetaskiwin, Alberta

The town of Wetaskiwin is a 35-mile drive south from Edmonton, Alberta, in the westernmost of Canada's prairie provinces. Although the community has a population of little more than 5000, it lies on the main highway between Calgary and Edmonton. It also boasts one of the more intriguing museums in western Canada, crammed with cars and trucks, fire engines, motorcycles, weapons, engines, and innumerable other items, including several vintage aircraft and a dozen aircraft engines.

The museum, which was originally founded in 1956 as the Western Canadian Pioneer Museum, is now known as the Reynolds Museum. Standing on 20 acres of property, the collection fills eight buildings. An extensive library on which work has been done for several years will eventually be open to the public.

The Reynolds Museum has well over 1000 vehicles and engines, as well as a varied collection of other items, including a number of Indian and Eskimo artifacts from various parts of western Canada.

Since the museum is connected to the local airport by a taxi strip, and new exhibits are being acquired regularly, plans call for starting flying shows within a few years. At the present time, the museum is only open five months out of the year, from the beginning of May through the end of September.

The half a dozen aircraft which may be seen include a 1940 Hawker Hurricane IIB and a 1917 Curtiss J–N4. The latter plane was used at Camp Borden, Ontario during World War I as a training aircraft. It was later owned by the City of Edmonton and used for various official purposes. The 1928 Gypsy Moth, equipped with both wheels and floats, was one of the early bush planes used in the northern part of the province.

The 1924 DeHavilland DH–60 Cirrus Moth was once owned by the Edmonton Aero Club and used for flight instruction. Also included in the collection are a 1929 Avro 594 Avian IV and a 1942 Fleet Cornell trainer.

A number of other items relating to aviation are on display, including some early fuselages and memorabilia relating to the Royal Flying Corps during World War I, as well as some machine guns of that period and early photographs.

A dozen aircraft engines are also on exhibit, starting with a 1912 Detroit Air-Cat two cylinder opposed, a 1916 Renault V-8, and 1916 a Hispano-Suiza V-8. Others are a 1928 Gypsy, 1920 Curtiss six cylinder, 1915 Gnome rotary, and a 1928

This Hawker Hurricane Mark IIB was restored during 1970 just thirty years after its original production year early in World War II. (Courtesy of the Reynolds Museum.)

Blackburn Thrush three cylinder radial. Engines from the 1930s and 1940s include Rolls Royce, Allison, Jacob, and Packard.

Location: The Reynolds Museum is located at the southwest edge of Wetaskiwin, the museum area connected to the airport by a taxi strip. There is ample parking space for automobiles, and visiting aircraft may taxi to within 300 feet of the museum building. Wetaskiwin is 150 miles north of Calgary and 35 miles south of Edmonton on Route 2A.

Schedule: Open daily from May 1 to October 1 from 10 a.m. to 5 p.m.

Admission: $1.50 for adults; $1.00 for students; 50 cents for children under 12 years; children under 6 years free. A 10 percent discount is available for groups.

The design of the Alexander Graham Bell Museum is based on the tetrahedral cell, used widely by the inventor both in constructing his early kites and in other engineering forms. (Photo by Frank Strnad.)

Alexander Graham Bell Museum
Baddeck, Nova Scotia

To generations of pupils, the name Alexander Graham Bell has been synonymous with the invention of the telephone. Yet, for almost a decade, he was one of the world's foremost aeronautical researchers, and many of the artifacts and papers displayed in the Alexander Graham Bell Museum bear witness to his engineering skills in this field.

Bell was a young man of 28 when he demonstrated the first successful telephone at Boston in 1875. His interest in aviation began to develop some 20 years later, prior to the turn of the century. His experiments with kites resulted in the accumulation of data on the principles of flight. He was convinced that a kite, if strong enough, could carry a man and an engine and achieve sustained flight.

In 1901, Bell developed the tetrahedral cell, a lightweight and extremely strong engineering construction. His man-carrying kite, the *Cygnet,* was tested in 1907. Towed by a steamer, it carried Lieutenant Thomas E. Selfridge of the U.S. Army on a successful flight.

Also in 1907, Bell and four others formed the Aerial Experiment Association, an organization which was to achieve considerable advances in aeronautical research and construct and fly four aircraft before being dissolved in 1909. Bell's associates in the group were Lieutenant Selfridge, Glenn H. Curtiss, John A.D. McCurdy, and W. F. "Casey"

269

Early kites, propellors, ailerons, and original drawings and plans, as well as models, are among the artifacts displayed in the Alexander Graham Bell Museum. (Photo by Frank Strnad.)

Baldwin. The Association had two headquarters, one at the Bells' Nova Scotia home near Baddeck and the other at Curtiss' motorcycle factory at Hammondsport, N.Y.

Aircraft developed by the group included the *Red Wing*, which made a flight of 319 feet in 1908 near Hammondsport; and the *White Wing*, which flew a distance of 279 feet at the same location a couple of months later. Baldwin made both flights.

The latter aircraft incorporated two innovations which represented significant contributions to aviation: the first ailerons, which provided practical maneuverability; and the first tricycle landing gear, which enabled aircraft to take-off and land without ground equipment for the first time.

The third aircraft completed by the group was the *June Bug*. On July 4, 1908, Curtiss won the *Scientific American Trophy* when he piloted the aircraft over a distance of one kilometer under test conditions for the first time.

This aircraft was later renamed the *Loon*, and pontoons were substituted for the undercarriage so that it was the first aircraft adapted to land on water.

On February 23, 1909, the group's largest and most advanced aircraft, the *Silver Dart*, was flown at Baddeck, the first flight by an aircraft in the British Empire. That flight covered half a mile, but a few days later, with McCurdy again at the controls, a flight of eight miles was made. A Silver Dart Memorial stands on the grounds of the museum in Baddeck today.

The museum itself contains early ailerons and propellors, and numerous original papers and drawings associated with the Aerial Experiment Association's work.

When the Association was dissolved, the same group formed the Canadian Aerodrome Company, the first aircraft manufacturing company in the country. Five aircraft were designed and built before the firm was disbanded.

The Bell museum is an attractive building situated on 25 acres of land across the bay from Bell's home. Its design is based on the tetrahedron and it was opened to the public in 1955. Organized groups visiting the museum can receive a lecture on Bell's work and the memorabilia exhibited.

In addition to aviation material, other exhibits cover Bell's work on acoustics and with the deaf, in communications, medicine, desalination, and hydrofoil boats, of which four were constructed and tested.

Location: Baddeck, Nova Scotia is situated in the center of Cape Breton Island in the northern part of the province, almost 50 miles by road from Sydney. From Route 105, the Trans-Canada Highway, Route 205, leads directly to the village of Baddeck. The Alexander Graham Bell Museum is at the east end of town and ample parking space is available.

Schedule: Open from 9 a.m. to 9 p.m. every day including holidays from May 15 to October 15. Open from 10 a.m. to 5 p.m. every day except holidays from October 16 to May 14.

Admission: Free.

Silver Dart Memorial commemorates the first flight made in Canada on February 23, 1909. John A.D. McCurdy piloted it on occasions for distances up to eight miles. (Courtesy of the Alexander Graham Bell National Park.)

National Aeronautical Collection
Ottawa, Ontario

It's easy for a visitor to the Canadian capital to come away with the impression that there are four aviation museums in the city. It's true that there are four places where one may view historic aircraft and artifacts, but in reality, all are part of a single National Aeronautical Collection, one which no serious enthusiast could term anything less than superb.

The National Aeronautical Collection was formed in 1964 when existing collections from the National Aviation Museum, the Canadian War Museum, and the Royal Canadian Air Force Collection were brought together at the Canadian Forces base at Rockcliffe near Ottawa, Ontario. The National Aeronautical Collection was absorbed by the newly-formed National Museum of Science and Technology in 1967. The Collection is administered through the museum's Aviation and Space Division.

The appearance of four museums in Ottawa stems from the fact that portions of the Collection are currently displayed in four different places. At the Rockcliffe base, a total of 88,000 square feet of space is utilized in three World War II hangars. There is an additional 18,000 square feet of space in use for aviation and space exhibits at the National Museum of Science and Technology on St. Laurent Boulevard, and some 4000 square feet of space devoted to military aviation in the Canadian War Museum. The fourth location is at the city's

Air shows and special events are often held at the Canadian Forces Base at Rockcliffe near Ottawa where three World War II hangars house most of the National Aeronautical Collection. Here an Avro 504K flies by during a vintage aircraft gathering. (Courtesy of the National Museum of Science and Technology.)

Uplands Terminal Airport Building, where 8000 square feet of space has been set aside for use by the National Aeronautical Collection.

The Collection contains a total of 92 aircraft and well over 200 engines. The objective of the Collection is to trace the development of aviation in both civilian and military applications, and, although there is some emphasis on Canadian history and technology, there is no effort to emphasize it exclusively.

Among the Collection's rarest aircraft are the sole surviving examples of the A.E.G. GIV and Junkers J-1 of World War I. Another aircraft of interest is the first aircraft ever used for exploration, the Curtiss Seagull used by the expedition of Dr. Hamilton Rice to the Upper Amazon River in 1924–1925.

In visiting the National Aeronautical Collection, it's well worth starting at the Rockcliffe facility and then making the six-mile drive south to the Museum of Science and Technology. Rockcliffe can be reached from the center of the city by driving north on St. Laurent Boulevard and turning right on Hemlock Road which leads to the entrance to the base. The Rockcliffe facility has no book shop, souvenir or gift counter, or restaurant. A couple of excellent small folders are available on the National Aeronautical Collection; one, in both English and French, includes a section of the history of aviation in Canada and illustrations and descriptions of about 30 of the aircraft contained in the collection.

Aircraft in the collection which are on display (using Canadian designations) are a replica of the AEA Silver Dart, first aircraft to fly in Canada; an AEG GIV; an Aeronca C-2; an Airspeed Consul; an Auster MK VI; an Avro Avian Mk IVM; an Avro 504K; an Avro Anson Mk V; an Avro CF–100 Mk IVB; an Avro Lancaster Mk X; a Bell HTL–6; a Bellanca Pacemaker; a Bleriot XI; a Boeing 247D; a Boeing Bomarc; a Bristol Beaufighter; a Bristol Bolingbroke Mk IVT; a Canadair DC–4M; a Cessna Crane; a Consolidated Canso Mk IISR; a Consolidated Vultee B–24L Liberator; a Curtiss JN–4; a Curtiss P–40 Kittyhawk Mk 1; a Curtiss HS–2L; a Curtiss Seagull; a deHavilland 82C Tiger Moth; a deHavilland 60 Cirrus Moth; a DeHavilland Mosquito Mk XXB; a DeHavilland Vampire Mk 1; a DeHavilland Vampire Mk III; a DeHavilland Canada DHC–1 Chipmunk; a Douglas Dakota

Mk IV; a Fairchild Cornell; a Fairchild FC–2W–2; a Fairchild 82; a Fairey Battle Mk II; a Fairey Swordfish; a Fleet 2; a Fleet 16Finch; a Fleet 50 and a Fokker DVII.

Also included are a replica of a Gibson Twinplane; a Hawker Hurricane Mk XII; a Hawker Sea Fury Mk XI; a Heinkel 162 Mk Al; a Junkers Jl; a Junkers W-34; a Lockheed CF–104; a Lockheed 10A; a Lockheed 12A; a Lockheed T–33; a McDonnell Banshee; a McDowall Monoplane; a Messerschmitt 163B; a Messerschmitt 109; a Nieuport 12; a replica of

The original engine which powered the *Silver Dart*, the first aircraft to fly in Canada, is displayed beneath a model of the plane. The flight was made on February 23, 1909, by J.A.D. McCurdy for a distance of half a mile over Baddeck Bay, Nova Scotia. (Courtesy of the National Museum of Science and Technology.)

Canada's National Aeronautical Collection contains numerous Royal Flying Corps and Royal Canadian Air Force and Navy aircraft spanning a sixty-year period. (Courtesy of the National Museum of Science and Technology.)

a Nieuport 17; a Noorduyn Noresman Mk VI; a North American Harvard Mk II; a North American Harvard Mk IV; a North American Mitchell Mk III; a North American P-51 Mustang Mk IV; a North American Sabrajet Mk IV; a Northrop Delta; a Piasecki HUP 3; a Pitcairn PCA-2; an RAF B.E.2c; a Sikorsky S51/H5; a Sopwith Camel 2F.1; a Sopwith Snipe 7F.1; a replica of a Sopwith Triplane; a Spad SVII; a Stearman 4 EM; a Supermarine Spitfire Mk IIB; a Supermarine Spitfire Mk IX; a Supermarine Spitfire Mk XVI; a Taylor E2 Cub; a Travelair 2000; a Vickers Viscount; and a Westland Lysander Mk III.

Location: The two principal locations of the National Aeronautical Collection are the Canadian Forces Base at Rockcliffe on Hemlock Road which can be reached on St. Laurent Boulevard, and the National Museum of Science and Technology which is at 1867 St. Laurent Boulevard in downtown Ottawa. The two other sites are at the Uplands

Terminal at Ottawa International Airport and in the Canadian War Museum in downtown Ottawa.

Schedule: All museum facilities are open from 9 a.m. to 9 p.m. seven days a week during the summer months, and are closed Mondays during the winter. Group tours are available by previous arrangement at the Museum of Science and Technology, but not at Rockcliffe.

Admission: Free.

APPENDIX

Organization and Publications

For anyone with a more than occasional interest in aviation, there are numerous organizations and publications of either special or general interest. Most organizations publish their own newsletters or journals, and several have state, local, or regional chapters which hold regular meetings.

There are organizations in the fields of military aviation, vintage aircraft restoration, soaring, aviation history, aircraft modeling, experimental aircraft, and others. Many do not limit their membership to pilots, engineers, or persons employed in the aerospace industries.

In addition, several of the aviation museums listed in this book are supported entirely by membership organizations which actively solicit public support.

The listing which follows is limited to organizations without specialized qualifications for membership. Most require only a genuine interest in aviation, aircraft restoration, or a related activity. In most instances, modest annual dues include subscriptions to informative newsletters and journals. Dues indicated are for individual memberships and may vary by age and other factors.

The second listing is of magazines devoted to aviation, and includes some publications which are available through membership in organizations. The list is one which has been selected for general, rather than professional, interest.

Organizations

Academy of Model Aeronautics
806 15th Street, N.W., Washington, D.C. 20005
Annual Dues: $12.00
Publications: *Aircraft Modeler, AMA News*

Aerobatic Club of America
2400 West 7th Street, Fort Worth, Texas 76107
Annual Dues: $15.00
Publications: *ACA News*

Air Force Association
1750 Pennsylvania Avenue, N.W., Washington, D.C. 20006
Annual Dues: $10.00
Publications: *Air Force Magazine*

Air Force Historical Association
910 17th Street, N.W., Washington, D.C. 20006
Annual Dues: $15.00
Publications: *Aerospace Historian*

American Aviation Historical Society
P.O. Box 99, Garden Grove, Calif. 92642
Annual Dues: $12.50
Publications: Quarterly Journal, monthly newsletter

American Helicopter Society
30 East 42nd Street, New York, N.Y. 10017
Annual Dues: $15.00—$20.00
Publications: *Veriflite, Journal of the American Helicopter Society*

Antique Airplane Association
P.O. Box H, Ottumwa, Iowa 52501
Annual Dues: $15.00
Publications: *Antique Airplane News, APM Bulletin*

Army Aviation Association
1 Crestwood Road, Westport, Conn. 06880
Annual Dues: $10.00
Publications: *Army Aviation Magazine*

Aviation Hall of Fame
Convention & Exhibition Center, Dayton, Ohio 45402
Annual Dues: $10.00
Publications: Quarterly newsletter

Canadian Aviation Historical Society
P.O. Box 224, Station A, Willowdale, Ontario M2N 588,
Canada
Annual Dues: $7.00
Publications: *CAHS Journal*, occasional newsletters

Experimental Aircraft Association
P.O. Box 229, Hales Corners, Wisc. 52130
Annual Dues: $15.00
Publications: *Sport Aviation*

International Aerospace Hall of Fame
Balboa Park, San Diego, Calif. 92101
Annual Dues: $5.00
Publications: Newsletter

Lighter-Than-Air Society
1800 Triplett Boulevard, Akron, Ohio 44306
Annual Dues: $6.00
Publications: *Buoyant Flight*

National Aero Club
16740 Highway 2818, San Antonio, Texas 87221
Annual Dues: $15.00
Publications: *Aero Magazine*

National Aeronautic Association
806 15th Street, N.W., Washington, D.C. 20005
Annual Dues: $10.00
Publications: *National Aeronautics, Journal of Aerospace
Education,* monthly newsletter

Naval Aviation Museum Association
Pensacola, Fla. 32508
Annual Dues: $10.00
Publications: None

Soaring Association of Canada
P.O. Box 1173, Station B, Ottawa, KIP 5AO, Canada
Annual Dues: $15.00
Publications: *Free Flight*

Soaring Society of America
P.O. Box 66071, Los Angeles, Calif. 90066
Annual Dues: $15.00
Publications: *Soaring*

Publications

Aero Magazine
P.O. Box 1184, Ramona, Calif. 96065
Frequency: Bi-monthly
Circulation: 85,000
Subscription: $4.00

Air Classics
7950 Deering Avenue, Canoga Park, Calif. 91304
Frequency: Monthly
Circulation: 150,000
Subscription: $5.00

Air Force Magazine
1750 Pennsylvania Avenue, N.W., Washington, D.C. 20006
Frequency: Monthly
Circulation: 107,000
Subscription: $7.00

Air Progress
437 Madison Avenue, New York, N.Y. 10017
Frequency: Monthly
Circulation: 126,000
Subscription: $6.00

Air Transport World
806 15th Street, N.W., Washington, D.C. 20005
Frequency: Monthly
Circulation: 45,000
Subscription: $8.00

Army Aviation Magazine
1 Crestwood Road, Westport, Conn. 06880
Frequency: Monthly
Circulation: 12,000
Subscription: $4.50

Astronautics and Aeronautics
1290 Avenue of the Americas, New York, N.Y. 10019
Frequency: Monthly
Circulation: 29,000
Subscription: $12.00

Aviation Week & Space Technology
1221 Avenue of the Americas, New York, N.Y. 10020
Frequency: Weekly
Circulation: 90,500
Subscription: $20.00

Business & Commercial Aviation
1 Park Avenue, New York, N.Y. 10016
Frequency: Monthly
Circulation: 57,800
Subscription: $10.00

Canadian Aviation
481 University Avenue, Toronto, Ontario, Canada
Frequency: Monthly
Circulation: 12,000
Subscription: $12.00

Canadian Flight
P.O. Box 563, Station B, Ottawa, Ontario, Canada
Frequency: Bi-monthly
Circulation: 9000
Subscription: $4.00

Canadian Wings
Building 15, International Airport, Calgary, Alberta, Canada
Frequency: Monthly
Circulation: 4800
Subscription: $5.00

Flight Magazine
2700 North Haskell, Dallas, Texas 75221
Frequency: Monthly
Circulation: 27,000
Subscription: $12.00

Flying
1 Park Avenue, New York, N.Y. 10016
Frequency: Monthly
Circulation: 386,000
Subscription: $7.00

Flying Models
31 Arch Street, Ramsey, N.J. 07446
Frequency: Monthly
Circulation: 31,000
Subscription: $6.00

General Aviation News
P.O. Box 1094, Snyder, Texas 79549
Frequency: Bi-weekly
Circulation: 33,000
Subscription:$3.95

Interavia Magazine
212 Fifth Avenue, New York, N.Y. 10010
Frequency: Monthly
Circulation: 55,000
Subscription: $17.00

Journal of Aircraft
1290 Avenue of the Americas, New York, N.Y. 10020
Frequency: Monthly
Circulation: 4000
Subscription: $10.00

Journal of Spacecraft & Rockets
1290 Avenue of the Americas, New York, N.Y. 10020
Frequency: Monthly
Circulation: 3700
Subscription: $12.00

Model Airplane News
1 North Broadway, White Plains, N.Y. 10601
Frequency: Monthly
Circulation: 80,000
Subscription: $7.25

Naval Aviation News
801 North Randolph Street, Arlington, Va. 22203
Frequency: Monthly
Circulation: 34,000
Subscription: $5.00

Scale Aircraft Modeler
7950 Deering Avenue, Canoga Park, Calif. 91304
Frequency: Bi-monthly
Circulation: 78,000
Subscription: $6.50

Soaring
P.O. Box 66071, Los Angeles, Calif. 90066
Frequency: Monthly
Circulation: 15,000
Subscription: $7.00

Plane & Pilot
P.O. Box 1136, Santa Monica, Calif. 90406
Frequency: Monthly
Circulation: 90,000
Subscription: $6.00

Rotor & Wing
PSJ Publications, Peoria, Ill. 61601
Frequency: Bi-monthly
Circulation: 32,000
Subscription: $8.50

Southern Wings
121 Candace Drive, Maitland, Fla. 32751
Frequency: Monthly
Circulation: 12,500
Subscription: $3.00

Space World Magazine
P.O. Box 36, Amherst, Wisc. 54406
Frequency: Monthly
Circulation: 10,000
Subscription: $8.00

Sport Flying
7950 Deering Avenue, Canoga Park, Calif. 91304
Frequency: Monthly
Circulation: 78,500
Subscription: $9.50

Vertiflite
30 East 42nd Street, New York, N.Y. 10017
Frequency: Bi-monthly
Circulation: 4000
Subscription: $10.00

Western Aviation/Airport News
11558 Sorrento Valley Road, San Diego, Calif. 92121
Frequency: Monthly
Circulation: 39,500
Subscription: $3.00